Temples, Tuk-tuks

Travels th

By Jason Smart

Text and Photographs Copyright © 2013 Jason Smart

All Right Reserved. No part of this book may be reproduced or transmitted in any form or by any means, electronic or mechanical, including photocopying, recording, or any information storage and retrieval system, without prior written permission of the Author.

First English edition published in 2013 by Smart Travel Publishing

Cover design by Ace Graphics

Smart, Jason J
Temples, Tuk-tuks & and Fried Fish Lips: Travels Through Asia

ISBN-13: 978-1492137818
ISBN-10: 1492137812

For my brothers Gary and Paul Smart

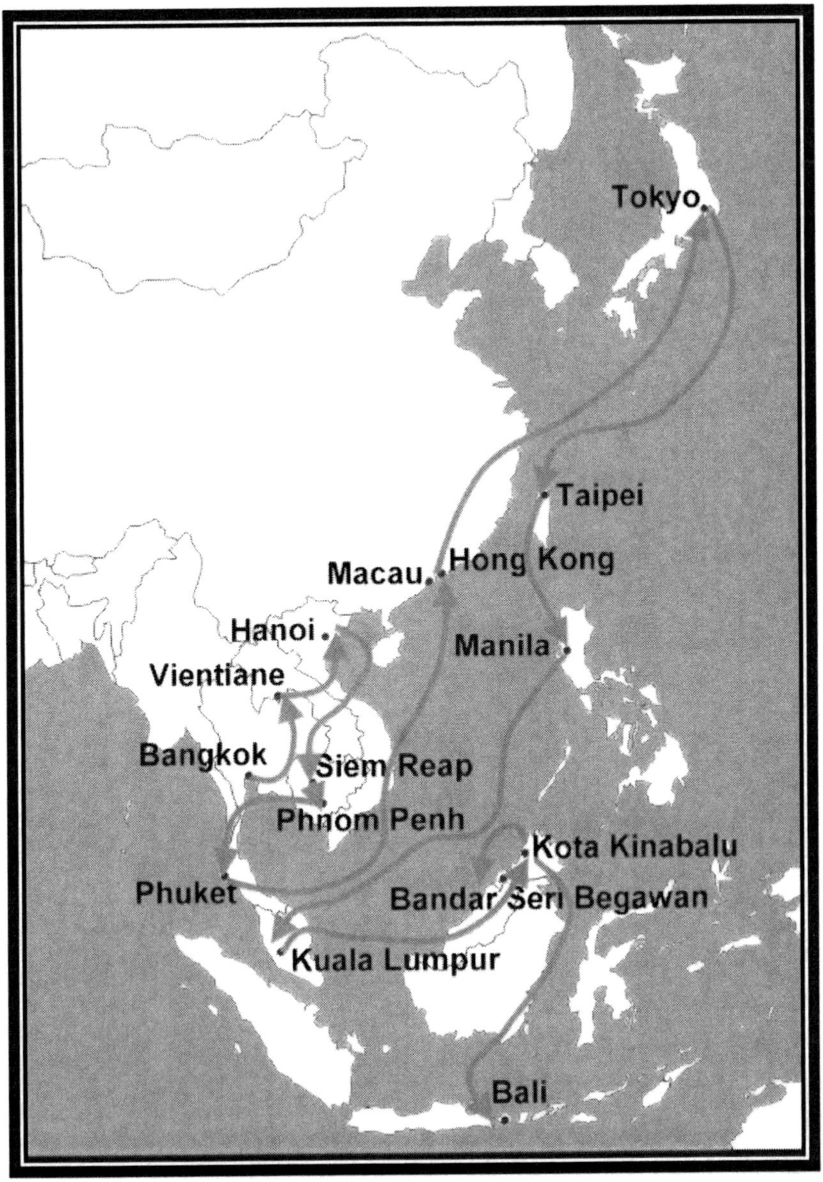
Tokyo
Taipei
Macau
Hong Kong
Hanoi
Manila
Vientiane
Bangkok
Siem Reap
Phnom Penh
Kota Kinabalu
Phuket
Bandar Seri Begawan
Kuala Lumpur
Bali

Table of Contents

Prologue 1

Chapter 1: You want Ping Pong? 3

Chapter 2. Vientiane - Not so sleepy 17

Chapter 3. Hanoi and Halong Bay 27

Chapter 4. Angkor Wat and the Floating Village 41

Chapter 5. The Killing Fields of Phnom Penh 53

Chapter 6. Beach Time in Phuket 69

Chapter 7. Hong Kong Phooey 77

Chapter 8. Sweating in Macau 91

Chapter 9. The land of the Robotic Toilets 99

Chapter 10. Fried Fish Lips in Taipei 111

Chapter 11. Onwards to Manila 121

Chapter 12: Kuala Lumpur, capital of Malaysia 135

Chapter 13. The Orang-utans of Borneo 145

Chapter 14. The Sultanate of Brunei 153

Chapter 15. Last days in Bali 163

Prologue

"Look at that thing," said Joe, our friendly Filipino taxi driver. "We call them rolling coffins." He was referring to the jeepney in front, a common sight in the Philippines. It looked like a cross between an old US school bus and a WW2 American jeep. Brow-wiping locals were sitting in the rear of the colourful vehicle, crammed together like sardines.

Angela and I were in the back of Joe's taxi as he drove us through the clogged-up streets of downtown Manila. We'd just arrived from Taipei and, though the flight had only taken a couple of hours, it had taken us to another world. Instead of order, there was chaos. Black smoke billowed from the jeepney's exhaust pipe (and the exhaust pipes of all the others jeepneys too), making the humid air seem more toxic. It was even worse than the smog of Bangkok. By the side of the road, pedestrians crowded around makeshift stalls that were selling fried food. Near them, lines of pedicab drivers stood chatting, oblivious to the pollutants entering their lungs. Their sidecar bicycles were doing a good job of narrowing the street even further.

Joe laughed. "They are not very safe, you know; backyard builders make the jeepneys by hand."

"Really?" I asked.

"Yeah. That's why I will *never* get in one."

Suddenly the jeepney in front stopped.

"Nincompoop!" Joe yelled, stepping heavily on his brake. "Stopping in the middle of the road like that! Total nincompoop!"

Angela and I smiled at the use of the word, no longer in common use in the United Kingdom. A passenger alighted from the back of the jeepney, quickly disappearing into the crowd. The vehicle moved off with a blast of smoke. A few moments later, we did too.

Asia was always exciting.

Chapter 1: You want Ping Pong?

"Please do not ride in tuk-tuk," said the taxi driver who picked us up at Bangkok International Airport. "Over sixty accidents every day involving tuk-tuk. You must take taxi, much safer."

We were heading into the city centre, driving along a modern highway. In the distance, the lights of downtown Bangkok shimmered in the humid night sky. Both Angela and I were dog-tired after such a long flight. Even the brief stopover in Dubai had done nothing to recharge our batteries.

Our hotel was on Silom Road, a busy thoroughfare consisting of upmarket hotels and financial headquarters; it was also close to the notorious Patpong red light district and night market. Despite our fatigue, we decided to have a wander.

Almost as soon as we stepped outside the hotel, I could feel droplets of moisture forming on my forehead. The air seemed thick with heat, almost overbearingly so. There was also the unmistakable smell of traffic fumes. I'd read that Bangkok was one of the most polluted cities in Asia, and as we walked along the tuk-tuk heavy road, I could see that this was perhaps true.

A few minutes later, we hit the beginnings of the night market. DVDs and wooden trinkets seemed the main items on offer, but there were plenty of clothes for sale too. People were everywhere, both tourists and locals. Young Thai girls sat outside certain establishments waiting for customers. But these were not the seedy sex dens of further along: these were the real deal, offering traditional Thai massages. They didn't appear to be getting much business, though, and the girls looked bored. The tuk-tuk drivers were doing better. They buzzed the street like colourful dragonflies, their occupants blithely unaware that they were apparently dicing with death at every turn.

"That picture looks nice," said Angela, stopping by a small stall. It was an eye-catching photo depicting three Buddhist monks walking over a wooden bridge. The haze in the background added to the effect.

"How much?" I asked the woman in charge. She didn't answer; instead, she picked up a calculator and typed in a price. She passed me the calculator.

I shook my head and handed it back. The woman typed in another figure. I looked and then showed it to Angela, who nodded. Price settled, we handed over some Thai baht and waited while the woman wrapped it up.

"Was she deaf, do you think?" asked Angela as we walked away.

"I'm not sure."

We carried on for a few hundred metres and arrived in Patpong.

2

Our trip to Asia had begun months previously in England.

"Where shall we go?" I asked my wife. "We've got almost seven weeks to fill."

Angela and I were staring at the huge canvas world map in our spare bedroom. It covered the entire wall, and little red dots littered it: the places we'd been. Apart from the Middle East, Asia was conspicuously empty.

Angela studied the map for a few moments, and then her finger rested on Japan. "I've always wanted to go to Tokyo."

I nodded. Tokyo was on my list too. Every time I'd seen it on TV, the Japanese capital had looked so sci-fi, so hi-tech. Tokyo would definitely be part of our itinerary.

"And these two." My wife's finger was switching between Bangkok and Hong Kong. "And I'd also love to see orang-utans in Borneo. That would be a dream come true. What about you?"

It was always an exhilarating feeling planning a new trip. The possibilities were endless, the costs potentially astronomic. We were lucky that our jobs allowed us two months' holiday in one go.

Without that benefit, there was no way we could undertake such a complicated and long journey. And on this particular trip, we wanted to visit as many different places as possible, getting snapshots of different cultures along the way.

"I like the sound of Tokyo and Bangkok. But I'd love to see Angkor Wat in Cambodia. And if we go there, then we might as well nip into Vietnam. Plus I'd like to visit Andrew in Manila."

"Oh yeah," said Angela. "We've got to meet Andrew. We promised him we would."

Andrew was an old colleague of ours who had moved to the Philippines about ten months previously. The last time I'd spoken to him, he'd insisted we head over there.

"And what about Kuala Lumpur?" I added. "And maybe somewhere in Indonesia." My head was spinning with the possible routes and travel permutations. "I know," I announced. "Let's go to all of them – or at least as many as we can in seven weeks. Let me draft out a rough itinerary and then we can take it from there."

3

"You want ping pong?" asked a wiry Thai man who approached from my left. "Good show!"

"No thanks," I answered. I'd forgotten my table tennis bat. The man disappeared, but a minute later, a different man sidled alongside. He proffered a piece of folded card towards me.

"Is menu!" he said, revealing a set of dirty brown teeth. As he rushed off into the crowd, Angela and I looked at it. As we'd suspected, it wasn't a restaurant menu: it was a directory of sex shows. Listings included *Pussy Smoke Cigarette*, *Pussy Fishes In*, and the mind-boggling *Pussy Magic Razorblade*.

"Do you know something?" I said to Angela. "Even if I was with a bunch of mates I wouldn't go and see a ping pong show. I just can't see the appeal. It sounds horrible."

"Yeah, right."

"No, really."

A tuk-tuk pulled up ahead of us. Two middle-aged Western men got out. One was bald, the other was fat: archetypal sex tourists. They paid the driver and headed into the crowded aisles and neon lights of Patpong Red Light District.

4

Patpong was busy. But it wasn't just middle-aged men wandering around – there were families too, and young couples. Patpong was a tourist hive. As we passed a girly bar (with gyrating young women just visible through the entrance), I noticed a Chinese family: Mum, Dad and two small children. Dad seemed the most interested.

We passed another neon-lit establishment, this time with semi-naked girls sitting outside on wooden stools. One gestured that I should go over. She didn't seem to mind I was with my wife. I waved her off and carried on walking. Bars had names such as Honey Club and Electric Blue. All of them were busy.

"Do you reckon any of them are ladyboys?" asked Angela as we passed another line of go-go girls. Again, some gestured towards us but most simply sat huddled in their skimpy attire, enjoying their own conversations.

"I don't know. It's hard to tell, and I'm not an expert."

A little further along, we saw a middle-aged white man surrounded by three young Thai girls. They were all sitting in a seedy little bar. One of the girls draped her arms over the man and whispered something in his ear. He nodded and put his hand on her thigh.

"Let's head down there," suggested Angela. We seemed to have come to the end of the main part of Patpong, but some red neon lights formed the start of what looked like another section. We crossed the road to get to it, and, more or less as soon as we did, three young men rushed up.

"You want Bangkok big cock?" one tout said with a wink. His T-shirt said he worked at an establishment called Dick's Cafe. I shook my head and waved him off. We passed another bar called Dream Boys. Young Thai men in tight clothes were sitting outside. I squeezed Angela's hand tighter. It was time to leave.

5

On the way back to our hotel, Angela decided to have an authentic Thai massage in one of the places we'd passed earlier. After perusing the menu on the window, she decided to have a foot massage. There was nothing seedy about the interior – in fact, it looked like a hair salon – and so we went in, following a Thai woman in jeans.

"Why don't you have a massage?" suggested Angela. "You'll be bored watching me for an hour."

"A massage? I hate them."

"Okay, be bored then."

Reluctantly I looked at the menu. Perhaps I would have something. I didn't really fancy a massage as such though (I found them unusually painful), but I spotted something that might do the trick.

While Angela's masseur got started with her feet, a young Thai girl led me to a nearby chair. After sitting me down, she reclined the seat and told me to relax. I did so as the woman covered my face in some sort of liquid. I then heard her tinkering with something on a nearby table. I closed my eyes as I felt the cold edge of the blade press against my skin.

Twenty minutes later, I had to admit it was the closest shave I'd ever had. My face hadn't felt as smooth since I was fourteen. Thanking the girl, I went to sit by Angela, who was only half way through her massage. I glanced back over at my shaver; she was busy cleaning the razor, allowing the blood to drip off before the next customer arrived.

6

The next day, after managing to sleep off most of our jet lag, Angela and I decided to visit Chatuchak Weekend Market. Braving the sweltering sun, we caught the efficient Skytrain, and were soon passing over the smog and gridlock of the roads below.

The market was a huge labyrinth of alleyways, crisscrossing each other in people-jammed junctions. The main aisles were in the open air, but the rabbit-warren side alleys were much more numerous and were all covered up. This meant the heat was intense, as was the smell. We waded into the throng, sweat erupting from every pore.

We passed endless clothes stalls but eventually came to a small section selling paintings. Artists sitting at tables with paintbrushes or pastels were producing art as we watched. Some of the pictures looked good.

"We can't buy anything," I told Angela. "We've only got a limited amount of space in the suitcases."

"I know," she said. "I'm just looking."

We moved on to the pet stalls. Cute puppies were either locked up in cages or on display inside large open-topped boxes. People stopped to stroke the most adorable ones, and this led us to speculate on the shelf life of a puppy, and what would happen once they had outgrown their sell-by date.

We walked past other stalls selling rabbits, hedgehogs, birds and tortoises, and I knew Angela would not be happy about it. She hated seeing animals cooped up in poor conditions. I remembered a few years previously, when our neighbours had bought a rabbit. They had kept it in the back garden in a hutch. At first, the family looked after the large floppy-eared rodent, but, as time passed, they began to ignore it. They still fed it, and gave it water, but they didn't bother letting it out of its hutch anymore. Whenever the family were out, and the coast was clear, Angela would creep into their garden and unlock the cage. With me keeping a good lookout, the rabbit would race around the garden, stopping occasionally to munch on some grass. After fifteen minutes or so, Angela would usher it back in and relock the latch.

"I can't stand it," she said, as we shuffled past a large tortoise crammed inside a box barely big enough to contain its body. "I need to get out."

And so, after sweating our way around Chatuchak Weekend Market for an hour, we found the exit and flagged down a pink Bangkok taxi. A minute later, we were heading towards the Grand Palace, previous abode of the King of Thailand.

7

Dazzling colours were everywhere: reds, whites and greens, but especially golds. Everything glittered in the sunlight. "This looks incredible," said Angela, as we wandered into a temple containing the famous Emerald Buddha. According to the leaflet we'd just picked up, it was one of the most sacred things in Thailand. It was old, too, dating from 43BC.

"It's a bit small," I said, pointing at it. Angela and I were jostling with all the other tourists inside the Temple of the Emerald Buddha. Placed high on a plinth stood the 45cm green Buddha. His face was green, but a golden costume covered the rest of him. As we tried to get closer, a man who worked in the temple noticed Angela.

"What you do?" the man yelled, flapping his arms. "Take off hat! Look what you do! Hat off!"

Angela removed her hat, feeling the stares of those nearby. She looked faintly embarrassed. I regarded the man. He looked like he was about to burst a blood vessel.

"No hat allowed inside temple!" the man shouted. "No hat!"

Okay, we get the message, pal, I felt like saying. Instead, though, we moved away from the Buddha.

"Naughty, naughty," I whispered to Angela. "I thought you'd smashed something the way he was going on."

"He was right though. I should've taken it off."

We stared up at the Buddha again. It looked intricately carved, but not interesting enough to make us want to linger. We made our way to the exit to collect our footwear.

8

A trio of orange-robed Buddhist monks were descending some temple steps. The Grand Palace was full of them, all young men with shaven heads, and robes wrapped around their shoulders and waists. I was slightly dismayed when one of them produced a mobile phone from somewhere. Monks with mobile phones? Somehow, it didn't seem right. But they still looked good enough for me to whip my camera out to take a photo.

We decided to catch a ferryboat back to our hotel. As we waited near a platform, we saw a young woman stroll over to a fence by the river. When she started tossing chunks of bread over the side, Angela and I went to investigate. The water was churning with fish. They were big ones too, writhing around with gaping mouths, flapping to get hold of the soggy bread. The woman noticed us staring and offered us some crusts. We politely declined and returned to the ferry platform.

"Is that our ferry?" I asked, watching as the small open-sided boat drew up alongside the jetty. It was already full.

"Come!" shouted a thin Thai woman who seemed to be in charge. "Walk on boat! Fill boat! Lots of room!" We did, and so did everyone else, squeezing for position on the narrow deck. We were soon powering away from the jetty, basking in the breeze created as we sailed downstream. A few minutes later, we pulled into another ferry stop where another bunch of people were waiting. When we docked, no one got off.

"Surely they can't get more people on?" I said to Angela. Already, everybody was pressed tightly together. It reminded me of being on the London Underground during rush hour. Once more, the small Thai woman in charge of checking tickets yelled for them to come aboard. "Move down boat! Lots of room! Come, plenty more people!" And somehow, even more passengers squashed themselves onto the already jam-packed vessel. It was a wonder we didn't sink.

9

The next morning, we headed for Wat Pho to see a gigantic reclining Buddha. Just inside the entrance to the complex, a teacher was leading a procession of impossibly cute five-year-old Thai girls. Each child was carrying a small cup of water and a toothbrush. Angela said she wanted to adopt one.

The golden Buddha was enormous. To reach its lower chin, we'd have needed a high ladder. Even his great golden feet towered way above our heads. As he rested upon one gigantic golden arm, his expression looked happy. He filled the whole room.

"This is better than the one we saw yesterday," said Angela.

I nodded in agreement. At 43-metres long, it was about the same length as a Boeing 737. It was infinitely better.

"So why is he reclining?"

"I'm not sure," I admitted, "but it must be to do with reaching Nirvana or something."

Back outside, I mentioned to Angela that I fancied going on another boat ride. "But not like yesterday," I said. "I reckon this time we hire a little boat for just the two of us. We can do a canal trip."

Angela looked at me. "We can do that?"

"I think so."

"Okay. But let's get some lunch first. I'm starving."

We headed away from the temple complex, passing an elephant with its owner. The huge mammal was munching on a pile of green leaves. On its head was an elaborate gold and red cloth, full of tassels and sparkly bits. On its back was a wooden chair. The man waved to us, wanting to know whether we were interesting in having a ride. We thanked him but shook our heads. Instead, we found a small restaurant near the Chao Phraya River.

10

"So what are your first impressions of Bangkok?" I asked as we sat down. Just across from us was the river: a fast flowing expanse of brown water busy with ferryboats. A few smaller boats were bobbing up and down on a nearby jetty, and wiry men smoking cigarettes were sitting near them playing cards. On the other side of the river was another spiky temple.

"I like it. It's more modern than I expected. I didn't realise there would be so many skyscrapers, though. But the temples are beautiful. And everything's so cheap. But the heat is strong. It feels so ...clammy."

Our food arrived, deposited by a thin woman wearing a streaked apron. We thanked her and tucked in. My chicken fried rice was delicious until I found the black hair. I pointed it out to Angela.

She grimaced and then shrugged. "Just leave it on the side of the plate."

I nodded and began to tuck in with less gusto. The presence of a hair in any meal had the power to do that, I'd noticed, but, as long as there were no fried lice in the fried rice, I supposed I could live with it.

"We're going to Laos next, aren't we?" asked Angela after swirling her fork around her plate to search out foreign bodies.

"Yeah. And then Vietnam after that."

A fly buzzed the table. No matter how many times I'd swiped at it, the insect would always return. It landed on a spoon we weren't using. I slowly picked up our Southeast Asia guidebook and hovered over it. As soon as I made a move to squash it, the insect flew away with ease.

"And after Vietnam we go to Phuket?" Angela asked.

"No. We fly to Cambodia first. By the way, do think this is actually chicken?" I was studying an unidentifiable piece of meat on my fork.

Angela looked at it, and nodded. "I'm pretty sure it is. But it's certainly not a prime cut. It can't be for the price we're paying. How much was all this?"

"Less than £1.50."

"Really? Including drinks?"

"Yes, plus a free pubic hair." I popped the piece of meat into my mouth.

11

Twenty minutes later, we felt brave enough to tackle the boat touts. Avoiding the card-playing men near the restaurant, we walked a bit further until we found some smaller boats. A man jumped up immediately. "You want river cruise?"

We nodded.

The man took a drag of his cigarette while appraising us. "Three thousand baht, for one hour," he said. "Very nice trip. You see many thing!"

I glanced at Angela and shook my head. Three thousand baht was more than sixty pounds. I looked back at the man. "Five hundred baht," I said. "For one hour."

The man laughed and dropped his cigarette in the water. There were plenty of others for it to join. In fact, the edge of the water looked like a rubbish tip. "Two thousand," he said.

I shook my head and took Angela's hand. We would try somewhere else.

"Okay, okay," the man said. "One thousand."

We nodded and boarded his narrow vessel.

12

The man lit another cigarette and started the outboard engine. Angela and I were sitting under a covered section in front of him, enjoying the breeze as we began to move along the river. Quickly, the boat turned into a much calmer side channel.

Houses on wooden stilts covered one side of the small canal. Men sitting on small wooden jetties were patiently holding onto fishing lines. We passed a dilapidated dwelling that was surrounded by dense green foliage, and, further along, we powered past a giant seated Buddha.

"This is nice," said Angela, leaning back in her seat to allow the wind to wash over her face. "This is the best bit of Bangkok so far."

Twenty minutes later, our boat slowed down. The driver switched the engine off and everything became quiet. "Fish," the man said.

We looked over the side and saw multitudes of large fish moving about. They were the same sort we had seen the day before. I asked the driver about them, wanting to know what type they were.

"Catfish," he said. "No eat!" He mimed being sick.

From the other side of the bank, an old woman in a small rowing boat approached. She spoke to our driver in thick Thai as she manoeuvred alongside us. Then she addressed us. "Bread for fish?"

I didn't know what she meant, but when she opened a large sack, we saw it was filled with pieces of bread. She gestured to the fish and then at her bread. "Bread for fish, yeah?"

After handing the woman a twenty-baht note, we received a pile of crusts, which we began to toss over the side. It was like a piranha attack. The water frothed and spun as the fish gorged themselves silly. While our driver lit another cigarette, the woman turned to a box in the back of her boat. From it, she produced a bottle of Singha Beer.

"Very cold!" she said. "You want beer?"

I was in such a good mood that I nodded, and bought one for the boat driver too. Angela opted for a bottle of water. Half an hour later, with the boat trip finished, the driver deposited us near Wat Arun, another of Bangkok's gloriously pointy Buddhist temples.

"Good trip?" asked the driver as we climbed out.

Both of us nodded. "Yeah, we really enjoyed it," said Angela.

"Great! Enjoy temple!" He lit another cigarette and went on his way.

13

In the UK, nobody would be allowed to climb the central tower of Wat Arun – Health and Safety would see to that. Sections of the stone staircase were almost vertical, and both of us had to pull ourselves upwards by using arm propulsion alone. Had we slipped, there was no doubt we would have tumbled to the bottom, breaking every bone in our bodies. But at the top, the views were worth it. On the opposite shore, we could see the Grand Palace in all its golden finery, and, by looking south, we could feast our eyes upon the jungle of skyscrapers. Bangkok was a real contrast of old and new.

"What time is our flight to Vientiane?" asked Angela as we surveyed the river. A large passenger boat seemed to be going sideways on it. It was a wonder it wasn't smashing into the smaller boats.

"Quarter past seven, this evening." I looked at my watch. "We'd better get moving, I suppose."

We carefully climbed back down the steps (which were even trickier on the descent) and studied the map. Our hotel wasn't far, we realised, and so we headed into Chinatown towards it.

Chinatown was a blaze of colour and humanity. Herbalists, spice shops, gold stores and noodle houses lined the busy street we were taking a short cut through. The traffic was hellish but the fumes were worse. No wonder so many of tuk-tuk drivers were wearing facemasks.

"I can't stand it," said Angela, scrunching up her face. "This air is killing my lungs."

I nodded in agreement. The atmosphere was thick with pollution and smoke. There was only one thing to do – we had to hire a tuk-tuk.

"Do you think we should?" Angela asked.

"Unless you want to suffocate..."

I stuck my arm in the road and one stopped within seconds. After bartering a price with the driver, we were off, weaving dangerously all over the road. The fumes were just as bad, but at least we had a breeze.

Beeeeep!

The shrill sound came from a large bus behind us. Our driver tried to squeeze into a space clearly not available to him.

Beeeeep!

This time it was from a taxi on our right. Our driver beeped his own horn, and swerved into another lane. Beside me, Angela gripped the metal bar: it was the only thing separating her from the madness outside. With a sudden burst of acceleration, we shot forward into a tiny gap ahead. By luck or judgement, we squeezed ahead of the jam. Ten minutes later, we arrived at our hotel safe and sound. Living on the edge was certainly cheap in Bangkok. The entire madcap ride had cost less than a pound.

We packed our suitcases in preparation for the next country on the tour: Laos.

Chapter 2. Vientiane - Not so sleepy

Angela and I knew the capital of Laos was going to be a lot quieter than Bangkok – the currency was called the kip for a start – but we saw the first real indication of how different things were on approach to Vientiane International. The night landing showed only a smattering of lights. It was as if we were arriving in a village.

The People's Democratic Republic of Laos (one of only five remaining communist countries in the world) liked its red tape. The airport was full of it. First, we had to line up to get our visa application forms, and then, once we'd filled them in, we were told to join a different queue for visa acceptance. A sombre man in a green military uniform, with epaulets full of gold stars, sat at the head of this new queue. He was checking people's passports. When we reached him, he took our forms and scanned the pages. He nodded and looked up. "Thirty five dollar," he barked. "Each."

We passed him the money, and he put it in a drawer already stuffed with US bills. After sticking visas in our passports, he sent us away. We then joined a third queue so we could get our passports stamped. People everywhere were joining queue after queue, wondering if they would ever be allowed to enter the country.

2

The streets of Vientiane were markedly quiet. Only a small number of vehicles were on the street with our taxi. A few neon lights suggested that the odd bar might be open, but it was a world away from Bangkok, or the 1960s, when the Americans had established Vientiane as an opium den and sex parlour.

After checking into our hotel, Angela and I decided to go for a little wander. As we made our way along an unlit street, we could hear the unmistakable sounds of the tropics: frogs and chirping insects. And then another sound broke through. Growling and yelping. Across the road, lit from a nearby bar, two stray dogs were fighting like mad. Two men from the bar stood up to see what was going on, and when they saw it was just dogs, they promptly sat back down.

The dogs were really laying into one another, twisting and grunting in their exertions. Then, suddenly, one broke free, running off into the shadows. The other dog stayed where it was, and then ran off in the opposite direction. The frogs and insects resumed their night-time soundtrack.

I spied a tiny store selling beer. Inside, four people were sitting at a table eating a meal – two adults, a teenage girl, and an old man. It crossed my mind that perhaps it wasn't a shop, and that we had walked into someone's home by mistake. All four were staring at us. The old man was holding his hand midway between his plate and his open mouth. He looked astonished, as if alien creatures had suddenly appeared in his dining room.

I was sure it was a shop, though. There were a few short aisles filled with tin cans and packets of rice, and there was also a glass-fronted fridge filled with Beer Lao. I pointed at it. "Can I buy some please?"

The family continued to stare but said nothing. By my side, Angela whispered that we should leave, but I went to the fridge and removed two bottles. I turned around and faced the people on the table. "Can I buy these?"

The most elderly member of the family finally came out of his stupor and walked over to me. He was eating the morsel of food that had been in his hand a moment ago. It looked like a bit of grasshopper. A second later, it was gone. He looked at the bottles and then spoke to me in a rapid-fire dialect that sounded vaguely Chinese. The people on the table resumed their eating.

"How much?" I inquired. The old man spoke again, this time with added hand gestures. From the gist of it, he was saying that I couldn't take the bottles away.

"Maybe we have to drink them in here?" I said to Angela. The man nodded and babbled away some more. Angela had a quick look around the store, and I could tell she didn't want to stay. I couldn't blame her; it was little more than a shack. I didn't want to stay either. There were no spare seats for a start.

I addressed the man speaking as slowly as I could. "Look, we want to take the bottles to our hotel. It's over there. Can we take them away, please?"

The man swivelled his head to where I was pointing, and then seemed even more confused. He said something to his family, which caused the whole lot to burst out laughing. I watched the old man's leathery lips tremble in amusement over a mouthful of missing teeth.

The stalemate was broken by the arrival of a younger man who entered the shop. After conferring with the old guy, the newcomer pointed to my bottles of Beer Lao. "This man, he say, you bring bottles here...after finish...okay...?"

Ah! It made sense now. The old man simply wanted the empty bottles back. I nodded like a prize galoot, which made everyone laugh even harder. We paid for the bottles and headed to our hotel. Our first interaction with the locals of Vientiane had gone remarkably well.

3

The next morning was another hot and humid one. Angela and I crossed a road on our way to see two of Vientiane's major sights: Patuxai (Victory Monument) and Pha That Luang – a famous Buddhist monument. Both were conveniently located along the same stretch of road.

The streets of Vientiane, although quiet, were not as laid-back as we'd expected. Sure, the city was no metropolis, but there were still plenty of tuk-tuks, motorbikes and cars on the road, giving

Vientiane a buzzing atmosphere. Toyotas seemed the vehicle of choice in the Laotian capital, most of them modern 4x4s.

"They should learn how to park them," I remarked to Angela as we made our way around a large white Toyota blocking a section of road and pavement. It wasn't the only one. "If they continue like this, in a few years this place will be gridlocked."

We arrived at some sort of shopping precinct. Most of the stores were selling cheap household goods, and outside one of the shops was a huge lizard. A couple of men were sitting on plastic chairs near it. Both looked up from their newspapers as we approached the reptile.

It was about five feet in length, with a long tail and jagged spines along its back. Because it was totally still, I wondered whether it was actually real. Perhaps it was a stuffed one, I thought. As I bent down to inspect it closer, the creature's tongue darted out. I jumped back in shock, stumbling over my own feet. As I got up, both men were laughing, and so was Angela.

"You're an idiot sometimes," she said.

4

The Patuxai Monument, also known as the Victory Monument, was easy to spot because it was massive. The giant arch stood in the middle of a wide boulevard. "It's like the Arc De Triomphe," Angela said as we neared Vientiane's best-known landmark.

Built in 1969, the Patuxai Monument had been commissioned by the Laotian government as a memorial to people who had died in battles prior to their communist takeover. A line of Laotian flags was by its entrance, as was a set of palm trees.

We were delighted to find we could climb Patuxai for a mere three thousand kip (15p). The ascent was relatively painless, as stalls had been set up on each floor. Old banknotes, flags, Beer Laos T-shirts and boxes with lids carved into the shape of elephants were all on offer. Angela bought some silk scarves from one peddler.

"£1.50 for all this!" she beamed after she'd completed the transaction. "This would cost a fortune in England."

The view from the top showed just how flat Vientiane was. And it wasn't particularly big either. We could see the whole city, and then the green expanse of jungle beyond. Below us, on the three-lane highway, the majority of vehicles were small motorbikes. We could hear their tinny engines, a sound we would get used to in South East Asia.

"Okay," I said. "That's sight number one ticked off the list. Let's head for number two."

5

Pha That Luang was a fair walk from Patuxai. The heat was hellish and I was sweating like a sweaty thing. Droplets of salty moisture ran down my forehead into my eyes. The bottle of water we'd brought was gone in seconds. The temperature was relentless.

"Watch out," warned Angela, but I'd already seen the gaping hole in the pavement. I sidestepped it easily.

"They should do something about these gaps," I said. "Imagine what it must be like at night. If you fell down that hole, you'd easily break an ankle."

As we approached the golden spire of Pha That Luang, something caught Angela's eye. It was behind some railings, and looked like an abandoned fairground. Everything was almost covered by overgrowth and leaves. Next to a rickety old Ferris wheel stood a large podium full of rusted bumper cars. Further in, creepers had started to devour a skeletal merry-go-round. "It's disturbing," said Angela. "It's like something from a horror film."

Pha That Luang looked magnificent though. The golden stupa, the holiest of all the Buddhist sites in Laos, looked like a gigantic golden cake with a big spiky bit in the middle. Up close, it didn't look quite as impressive. It needed a lick of golden paint to cover the scratches and gashes. We had the stupa to ourselves, however; the crowds that should have been present at such a major monument were simply not there. For a while, we wandered the temple unhindered by anyone.

"So that's both sights of Vientiane done then," I said, wiping my forehead with my hand. "And it only took us an hour and a half."

6

As we left the stupa complex, a woman holding two small wooden cages approached us. Inside each cage was a pair of tiny birds. It was obvious what she wanted: money so that we could release them.

"This is so cruel," whispered Angela. "And I know we shouldn't, but I want to let some go."

I nodded, handing the woman 17,000 Kip (just over a pound). In return, she gave us one cage. Inside, two birds were chirping happily to themselves, unaware of what was happening. Angela didn't look remotely happy, though. We knew that by giving money to the woman we were perpetuating the cruelty to these small creatures.

"I just hope they don't get caught again." Angela lifted a small wooden latch and the birds flew away.

"Well at least they're free for now," I said, watching them disappear.

We decided to hire a tuk-tuk for the journey back to our hotel. There were two of them parked close to the Pha That Luang, but only one of them had a driver. He was in the back, asleep on a makeshift hammock. After we politely coughed in his direction, the man awoke and jumped to attention. A minute later, we were bouncing around in the back, gripping on for dear life, passing the occasional orange-robed monk. Soon we were calming ourselves in the hotel pool. We were the only people there.

7

Later that afternoon, we decided to walk to the mighty Mekong. Small bars and local eateries were set up on wooden scaffolds at the edge of the river. We entered one, making a perilous journey across a rickety wooden plank that shook and bounced as we gingerly stepped along it.

Enjoying another Beer Lao, with a vista spanning the Mekong, was a good way to spend a short while. Among some nearby rushes, Angela spotted a small canoe. It emerged, containing three fishermen. As we watched, they cast their small nets into the murky waters and waited. A few minutes later, the men moved on, passing where we were sitting.

"Oh my God," screeched Angela, pointing at my T-shirt. "What's that?"

I looked down and saw it. A massive green bug had just landed on me. It looked big enough to eat a finger, and so I stood up, hoping it would drop off.

"It it a locust?" asked Angela, keeping well back.

"I don't know, Angela. Maybe you can pass me my magnifying glass and callipers so I can study the specimen up close."

I shook my shirt but it resolutely refused to budge. Instead, it stared at me with its hideous orange eyes. Then it started to walk up towards my neck.

"Errr!" shouted Angela. "Do something!"

I already was: I was dancing a jig, jumping around in circles, realising I had no choice but to pick the thing up. A man who worked in the bar rushed out to see what all the commotion was about, and then laughed when he saw what it was. Tentatively, I made a grab for the beast, but backed off at the last second. My hand had scraped one of its hideous feelers. Then, just as sudden as its arrival had been, it was gone, buzzing off towards the Mekong.

"Tell me again," asked Angela a few minutes later. "What are our plans for the next few days? I know you've already told me a hundred times, but I just want to know about the next week or so."

"We're here for one more night, and then we fly to Hanoi tomorrow evening. We'll be in Vietnam for three days, and one of those days is set aside for our trip to Halong Bay." Halong Bay had been Angela's idea. She had seen a program about it on TV, and insisted we go. "After that, we fly to Siem Reap in Cambodia. We've a tour of Angkor Wat organised. Then we go to Phnom Penh."

"That's the capital of Cambodia, right?"

"Yeah. We can visit the Killing Fields there. It won't be much fun, but I think it's something we need to do. And then we fly to Phuket for a bit of beach and relaxation before the next segment begins."

Angela gazed out across the brown Mekong. Every so often, a white bird would fly into view before disappearing into the reeds.

"We're so lucky, you know," she said. "Being able to do all this."

I nodded and smiled. "I know."

8

That evening, I returned the empty bottles to the store across the road. Inside was a young girl of about fourteen. I didn't recognize her, and she, in turn, looked confused when I handed the bottles over. She put them on the counter and looked at me strangely. Faintly embarrassed, I left the shop and returned to the hotel. But at least I'd kept my side of the bargain.

The next afternoon, we caught a taxi back to the airport. Our brief stay in Laos was almost at an end.

"I hope you have enjoyed your stay in my country," said the jovial taxi driver.

We told him we had. Angela then asked him about the abandoned fairground we'd seen the previous day.

"Ah yes, fairground! It owned by government. It used to be popular place. But now no good." The man looked pensive for a moment before speaking again. "My government is good at building new projects, but not so good at maintenance. When people stop going to fairground, it quickly fall apart. The government will knock it down soon. They will use land for something else."

"Like what?" Angela asked.

The man shrugged. "I do not know. The people of Laos never know. We see construction all the time, but we do not know what is being built. The government never tell us. That is the way of the communists. But we can't really complain. The government have done much good for Laos. For one thing, there is no war anymore. I born in 1966, and remember things during war. Not good."

We reached the airport and said goodbye to the taxi driver. We gave him all our remaining kip, knowing we wouldn't be able to change any of it once we left. He thanked us graciously. It was time to leave Laos and head to Vietnam.

Chapter 3. Hanoi and Halong Bay

Our night flight from Vientiane to Hanoi was supposed to take less than one hour, but it ended up taking much longer.

A tropical storm was brewing over Hanoi, causing havoc with air traffic in and out of Noi Bai International Airport. As we sat on board the Vietnam Airlines Airbus, we didn't know this. Instead, we merrily ate the strange gelatinous objects the cabin crew had delivered to us.

"What is it?" asked Angela, wobbling a cylindrical piece of white stuff. It was about the thickness of a pencil, but the length of a thumb. She replaced it on her tray.

"No idea," I answered, sniffing mine. It didn't smell of anything and so, without further ado, I bit a chunk off. It tasted of nothing in particular, and, after rolling it around with my tongue for a moment, I chewed and swallowed.

Angela was grimacing. "If you don't know what it is, how can you eat it?"

I shrugged, picking up a wobbly pink thing next. It looked like a piece of jelly. After a quick nibble, I deemed it bland and so put it down on the tray as well.

As we began our night-time descent into Hanoi, the first indication that not all was well came from the turbulence. The *Fasten Seatbelt* signs had been on for quite some time now, and the bumps were getting worse. I peered outside, but all I could see was the aircraft's navigation strobe on the wingtip. It looked like it was dancing. The wing was undulating like a seesaw.

Down we went, but the flight crew aborted the landing at the last second. As the jet engines screamed up to full throttle, we climbed through the hot, turbulent air, buffeted on all sides by the storm outside. As the aircraft stabilised, an eerie sense of unease settled over the cabin. All of us had seen movies just like this.

No announcement came from the cockpit, and the cabin crew remained deathly quiet, strapped in at the front. By my side,

Angela whispered that she was scared, and then, with a sudden jolt, I was too. The jet dropped and my stomach remained thirty feet above me. I felt a sickening feeling in my chest, but then the plane righted itself once more.

The flight crew prepared the jet for a second approach, descending into the troubled lower altitudes. Outside was nothing but murk, only the occasional muffled flash from lightning in the distance. Suddenly the aircraft made a terrifying lurch to the left, and, from behind us, a woman screamed. A second later, the engines spooled up once more to full power. The landing had been aborted a second time. We climbed into the sky with the overhead bins rattling in frustration. They were the only sound apart from the screaming.

Actually, I made the last bit up, but you get the picture. We ended up circling over Hanoi for another fifteen minutes before the pilots sensibly diverted to the coastal town of Da Nang. An hour later, we were on the ground, safe and sound.

2

Neither of us had ever heard of Da Nang, but we quickly found out it was Vietnam's third-largest city, located half way between Ho Chi Minh City and Hanoi.

From the airport we were bussed, all one hundred and seventy of us, to a plush hotel in the centre of town. For some of the young backpackers on board the flight, this was like winning the lottery. Two Irish girls sitting behind us whooped for joy when they saw the hotel. "We were going to pay two dollars for a hostel! This place will have showers!"

We didn't see much of Da Nang because we had to be up at four the next morning. But from the top floor of the hotel, it looked pleasingly Asian. Its low-rise skyline was a sprawl of pink, green, yellow and blue, and in the distance, towering above the horizon, were some brooding mountains. Da Nang was a place we might return to one day, Angela and I agreed.

We eventually got to Hanoi at 9.30am. Though the storm had gone, it was still overcast and humid. Despite our weariness, our first port of call was Hoan Kiem Lake.

3

The lake was a large expanse of green water surrounded by shops, cafes and restaurants. As we traversed its southern edge, Angela asked me what was so special about it.

"Well," I said, reading from the guidebook, "according to some legend, a 15th century emperor was celebrating by having a sail over the lake. While he was doing this, a golden turtle appeared from the depths. It stole his sword, and swam back down."

"And...?"

"And that's it, I think."

We found an ATM and I put my card in. The lowest amount I could get out was 100,000 dong (£3). I pressed the button to get three million. Out popped a bunch of notes with Ho Chi Minh's portrait gracing the front, his wispy beard easily recognisable.

The lake was clearly a focal point for the citizens of Hanoi. People of all ages were wandering along its edge or sitting on one of the many benches surrounding it. There were even a few keep-fit classes going on. We passed one group of exercisers, mainly elderly people, all swaying and bending in time to some music blaring out from a battered speaker in a tree. But the biggest group of people around the lake were teenage couples. Many of them were canoodling underneath hanging branches or walking hand in hand. The lake was a love nest.

The old part of Hanoi was located to the north of the lake. To get there, we had to cross a busy road, which was easier said than done. There were pedestrian crossings, but they might as well have been invisible. Every vehicle simply ignored them. There was only one thing to do: we had to follow the example of the locals.

4

We stepped off the pavement and walked out. Slowly, but confidently, we took one step at a time, keeping eye contact with the oncoming traffic. Like rocks in a river, the traffic flowed around us. Sometimes the motorbikes were only inches away.

"I don't like this," said Angela between gritted teeth. I nodded and clutched her hand more tightly as we kept up our slow and steady walking pace. Every driver approaching us was calculating a trajectory based upon our predicted movement. If we suddenly stopped, or speeded up, it would throw the whole system into disarray. And so we kept going.

We reached the other side of the road and breathed a sigh of relief. We were in a busy area of beeping, beeping and more beeping. Motorbikes and cyclos were forcing their way through the already-crowded streets of the old town. Neither of us had ever seen so many motorbikes in any one place. Lines of them were parked by the side of the road, but many more were zipping along, their small engines causing a racket.

We came to an intersection, where a platoon of peddlers stood selling shoes, hats, watches and fruit. Wandering among them were conical-hat wearing women. They carried horizontal sticks over their shoulders, pots dangling from each end. Some of the pots had bundles of clothes in them, others had fruit. One woman seemed to be carting just litter. We carried on past them until we arrived at a small section of the old town dedicated to the sale and repair of shoes, and, further along, a small street devoted to the construction of gravestones. But then Angela spotted a silk shop and decided to go in. "It'll be expensive," she said, opening the door. "But I'll just have a quick look."

Twenty minutes later, she had been measured up for a dress and an underskirt. "I can collect it in two days. A fitted silk outfit! It's gorgeous! And only thirty dollars!"

That was the thing about South East Asia – it was so bloody cheap.

5

Later that evening, things were not so cheap.

Sick and tired of the noodle shops and street food we'd been eating in Bangkok and Vientiane, Angela and I decided to splash out and dine at a proper restaurant for once. The one we chose was Bobby Chinn's, an upmarket restaurant catering for, as far as we could tell, a mainly western clientele. It looked grand from the outside, and plush from the inside. As we were ushered to our seats by a well-dressed waitress, we couldn't help but be impressed. We sat down and perused the menus. Eventually we both ordered the salmon.

"This is raw," said Angela twenty minutes later.

I looked as she showed me the red flesh in the middle. Even to my untrained eye, I could tell it was not cooked. I cut into my own salmon and found it in the same state. The outside of the fish was pink and cooked, but the middle was stringy and red.

Angela and I never complain in restaurants; it's simply not in our nature. But with Bobby Chinn's charging an arm and a leg for our meals, I was ready to complain for the first time in my life. When the waitress approached, asking if everything was to our liking, I shook my head. "No," I stated. "Our salmon's raw. Look."

The young Vietnamese waitress's smile disappeared immediately. She bent down to inspect my plate, and then straightened up. "No, sir. It is not raw. It has been smoked for five hours before cooking. It is delicious. There is nothing wrong with your salmon." She forced a smile and, at the same time, gave me a look reserved for heathens of fine dining.

I poked about in the fish with the waitress watching every move. The inside was red and uncooked; it was plain to see. I pointed at a raw section again. "So you're telling me this is cooked?" Angela looked embarrassed, but I was undeterred.

The waitress smiled a most condescending smile. "Yes, it is cooked," she repeated. She might as well have added, *'Why are you here? It is clear to me, and all the other diners in this restaurant, that you are far too uncouth to be in an establishment such as this. Please take your wife and leave by the back entrance. We will place your food in a large trough in the alleyway.'*

I looked at the salmon and then at the waitress. She smiled and said, "Will there be anything else?" I shook my head. She gave a small bow and walked off.

I looked at Angela. "Well that went well."

Despite its uncooked middle, we still ate the food. For the price we were paying, I felt like eating the cutlery as well. With a bitter aftertaste in our mouths, we left the restaurant, wondering what Mr Chinn would make of our experience. Not a lot, I thought.

6

"It wasn't that bad," said Angela, as we flagged down a cyclo driver to take us back to our hotel. It was dark, and I could see some laser lights shining from the other side of the lake. They were thin beams of white going vertically upward from the lake temple. "And it was quite tasty. Besides, people eat raw salmon all the time."

"Not when they've ordered it cooked. Anyway, we're going to that cheap restaurant down the road from our hotel tomorrow. I can't face Bobby Chinn's again."

Neither of us had been in a cyclo before (a three-wheeled pushbike with a double seat at the front), and when we climbed in, it felt decidedly flimsy. A tuk-tuk was a tank compared to this. After negotiating a ridiculously low price with the driver, he pedalled out into the road. To be among the thick of Hanoi's traffic was exciting as a pedestrian, but, in a slow moving bicycle, with only a tiny metal bar as protection, it was exhilarating, especially at junctions where every powered vehicle skimmed past us, beeping their horns.

I turned around to speak to the middle-aged man pedalling away, asking if he was tired. The man grinned. "Me, tired? No! I no get tired. I pedal for one hour and no get tired!"

Fifteen minutes later, he dropped us off at the hotel. I gave him his money and added a tip.

"Many thanks," he beamed. "I very glad!"

7

The next day was an early start. We were driving to Halong Bay, famous for its limestone mountains. A guide called Tang picked us up from the hotel. He was a stocky man in his late-twenties with a friendly smile.

The journey, Tang told us, would take three hours by car, but the time would pass quickly because of the scenery outside. He was right. It was the Vietnam we'd imagined before arriving in Asia. Farmers were working the lush and verdant paddy fields. Water buffalo were grazing by the side of the road, their huge, curved horns looking capable of piercing armour. The countryside of Vietnam was beautiful.

Towns were a different matter. We passed through one untidy settlement, which had a massive white building emblazoned with a giant logo of Canon, the Japanese electronics giant, on the front. Tang noticed us staring and spoke up. "This area used to be paddy fields belonging to local farmers. They grew rice to sell, and to feed their families with, but then foreign companies came. Not just Canon – there were lots of others too – and our government sold the land to them." Angela and I stared outside. Ugly construction work had spoilt the natural scenery. Factories and poor-quality buildings had replaced green fields.

"The government paid off the farmers, and at first they were happy. They were suddenly rich." Tang paused, regarding the scene outside. "But farmers are uneducated men. They soon spent all the money and had no way of feeding their family anymore. Their land is gone; they cannot grow rice, and soon the family is hungry again. These farmers are a big problem for my government."

8

The road to Halong was full of beeping traffic. Most vehicles thought nothing of swerving into the wrong lane at the last second to overtake. But at least the speed we drove at was relatively slow. It had to be, with the sheer number of cars, lorries and motorbikes travelling along the highway.

A motorbike in front was proving to be problematic, though. Balanced on its rear end were a set of wire cages containing chickens. There must have been at least fifty hens in them. And further along, blocking one lane of traffic, was a cart being pulled by an ox. Eventually, we passed them, and carried on with the journey.

As we drove through another small town, Tang pointed at some houses. Most looked unfinished; all bare concrete and gaping holes where the windows should have been. "Builders make the shell of the houses," Tang explained. "Then sell them. As you can see, some have been bought and completed."

Completed wasn't the word I'd have used. Granted, the fronts looked magnificent, all ornate and colourful, but the sides were still bare concrete. It was as if the owners had only enough money to finish a partial section of their new homes. For the briefest of seconds, their houses looked top notch, but as soon as the angle changed, and the concrete sides became visible, they looked unfinished and drab. "And the reason they are so thin," said Tang, "is because our government collects tax based on the width of a building."

We drove onwards towards our destination.

9

Halong bay looked amazing. The sort of place you might see on a photograph, and promise yourself that one day you will go there. The harbour was a nest of colourful, wooden boats with tall masts, all waiting for tourists to board them. Many of the tourists were wearing rain-protecting plastic bags.

"You want rain coat?" asked Tang.

I looked at Angela. The rain didn't seem that bad, and besides, in the heat, it was actually quite cooling. We decided to pass on the bags.

Beyond the boats, out at sea, was the main draw of Halong Bay – magnificent limestone hills that rose from the sea like mythical mountains. Cloaked in green, hundreds of the formations towered above the water. They looked like the setting for a fantasy movie. The name, Halong Bay, translated as Bay of Descending Dragons, and the scene we were staring at looked stunning, even with an overcast morning.

We boarded our boat, soon setting off across the emerald sea. As we sailed between two of the huge limestone hills, a fish eagle flew alongside us. After a graceful tilt of its wings, it swooped towards the surface of the water. It came up with a silver fish in its talons.

Angela and I were surprised we were the only two passengers aboard the boat, even though it could probably hold fifty or more people. Tang told us it was due to the weather, and because not many people came to Vietnam in the wet season.

The wet season in Vietnam (like most of Southeast Asia) lasts from July to October. Typically, mornings will be sunny, with sporadic but torrential downpours in the afternoon and evenings. This explained our terrifying flight into Hanoi a few days previously.

We pulled alongside a floating fish market. Lobsters, shrimps, blue crabs and large fish were on show inside large tanks.

"Yu-ba-lobsta?" asked a small woman in charge of the market. She said the question so quickly that it took me a moment to work out what she meant. Did I want to buy a lobster? I shook my head and smiled. What would I do with it for a start?

A small boat slowly passed us. Washing hung from its wooden frame, and two small boys were sitting on the narrow deck eating rice from a white bowl. A teenage boy was in charge of steering, using two long wooden oars to keep the vessel steady. Mum and Dad were at the front with fishing nets. The woman was crouching in that distinctly Asian way. Her knees were bent to her armpits as she balanced on the very lip of the boat. I'd tried to sit like that once, with disastrous results.

We climbed back aboard our boat and headed for the Dong Thien Cung Cave, an area of Halong Bay flanked by dense green jungle. A short while later, we pulled up alongside a jetty and disembarked.

10

"It was discovered by a policeman," Tang told us as we climbed some steps to reach the mouth of the cave. "He was chasing a monkey but then lost sight of it. When he investigated, the man found a hole in the hillside. It was a huge cave."

The large cavern looked stunning; the ambient lights were highlighting a gaping mouth of stalagmites and stalactites that seemed to stretch in all directions. It was as if we were inside a dragon's jaws. Water dripped atmospherically from the huge roof; one stray droplet landed on my neck and travelled down my back.

"See that rock formation over there?" said Tang, pointing to a large piece of limestone that looked like a gigantic breast. "What does it look like to you?" Tang looked at Angela, then me.

Angela had the first guess. "Erm...some kind of turtle?"

Tang smiled. "Good guess, but you are not correct. What does it look like to you, Mr Jason?"

I coughed, stalling for time. I couldn't very well say, *'Well Tang, it looks like a great big woman's tit. It even has a nipply bit jutting out the top. By the way, I enjoy molesting bats. Do you know where I can buy some?'* Instead, I rubbed my chin, desperately trying to come up with something plausible.

"Hmmm...Is it a dragon?" It was as good a guess as any.

Tang shook his head. "No, it is not a dragon. It is a woman's breast. It even has a stalagmite that resembles the nipple. By touching this rock it will bring good fertility to women."

11

"I really enjoyed Halong Bay," I said, as we settled back in the car for the return journey to Hanoi.

Angela nodded. "The boat ride was the best bit."

Suddenly, there was a roar of thunder outside. Almost immediately, a sheet of rain lashed against the windscreen, drowning out any forward vision. As localised flooding began, everyone outside produced thin plastic sheeting to cover themselves with. Motorcycles zipped through deep puddles, leaving high arcs of spray in their wake. Another of Vietnam's tropical storms was underway.

Twenty minutes later, it was dark and the storm continued. Flashes of lightning silhouetted the horizon briefly as the wipers went hell bent for leather. Our driver was concentrating hard, that was plain to see. Many of the motorcycles and small trucks we were overtaking had no lights. How we didn't hit any of them was a miracle. When we arrived in Hanoi a few hours later, the place was flooded; the streets awash with rivers of brown water. Tang dropped us off at the hotel entrance, where we said goodbye and shook his hand. We then ran at top speed through the doors, stepping into the foyer like drowned rats, even though we'd been outside for less than ten seconds. An hour later, we decided to get something to eat.

12

"Oh my God!" cried Angela, as the cyclist went sprawling over the bonnet of our taxi. The man tumbled onto the soaked road. All three of us sat in silence; only the incessant sound of the raindrops spattering the windscreen could be heard over the idling car engine.

A minute previously, our taxi driver had been doing a U-turn in the road. Angela and I were returning to the hotel after our evening meal. The darkened streets were slick with rainwater. It was during the U-turn that the collision had occurred.

"Oh my God," Angela said again, straining forward to see how badly injured the cyclist was. And then a surprising thing happened. The cyclist simply got up, brushed the excess water from himself, and rubbed his head. While we watched in amazement, the young man picked up his bike, and, after deeming it undamaged, climbed on and began pedalling away. Our driver shrugged and engaged first gear. Without a word, he continued his U-turn, and then pulled up outside the hotel. Running down a cyclist was apparently an everyday occurrence in downtown Hanoi.

13

The next morning, it was still raining. It was coming down in great big, greasy blobs of water, which soaked our clothes to the skin. So much for mornings being sunny, I thought. We joined the queue to see Ho Chi Minh's embalmed body, trying our best to keep dry, but failing dismally.

As we shuffled forward in the snaking line, a group of people bypassed us and went straight to the front. All were men in their sixties wearing some sort of old green uniform. Most of them wore medals.

"They must be veterans from the war," I said. "So I think we'll let them off." In fact, I was pleased that they had pushed to the front. They had surely earned the right.

Two white-uniformed guards stood to attention at the entrance to the mausoleum, each with a bayonet-tipped rifle. We filed in, feeling the chill in the air as soon as we did so. Quickly, we arrived at the tomb room. Two large red flags adorned the rear wall: one of them, a gold star on a red background, was the flag of Vietnam; the other featured a golden hammer and sickle, the sign of communism. Four guards stood to attention around the body of Ho Chi Minh, his wispy beard there for all to see. As we slowly walked around his glass enclosure, it reminded me of seeing Lenin's embalmed body. As in Moscow, the waxwork appearance of Uncle Ho made it hard to believe we were looking at an actual dead man. Ten seconds later, we were out, back into the rain, back into the heat.

We flagged down a cyclo to take us to the silk shop. After collecting Angela's green silk outfit, we caught another cyclo to the hotel. The third country on our Asian adventure was finished. It was time to head to the airport for our flight to Cambodia.

Chapter 4. Angkor Wat and the Floating Village

As Angela and I descended into Siem Reap, we could see a flat landscape of green fields and waterlogged floodplains. Occasionally we'd catch glimpses of small settlements, but mostly, the vista outside was one of countryside.

The aircraft made a gentle landing and we taxied to the terminal. The sun was shining and the afternoon was bright. Both of us were thankful to have left the rain behind in Hanoi. The airport was modern and highly efficient. Passport and visa control went smoothly and we were soon on our way into town.

"It looks like a boom town," I said, as we drove though the outskirts of Siem Reap. "It's like those gold rush towns of the American Midwest." Construction was going on everywhere. The town was not the sleepy backwater we were expecting; no, this was a thriving place in the grip of tourist fever. Brand new hotels were everywhere, some of them 5-star. The Japanese had funded the roads, the Germans had helped restore the temples, and all around was the scent of a dollar to be made.

2

That evening, while Angela went for a back massage, I got talking to an American man sitting next to me in a busy bar.

Chuck was a wiry, fifty-something ex-pat from Texas. He had travelled the world on his motorbike, he told me, and was now living in Siem Reap. I asked him how long he'd been in town.

"Oh, now there's a question," he answered, his thick Texan drawl curling every word. "I guess it's been eighteen months now." Chuck seemed to ponder this. "Hell, that's a long time; it's about time I packed up and moved on. Don't wanna grow roots now."

I asked him where he'd lived before coming to Cambodia. He took a sip of beer before answering. "Let's see. I worked in Kuwait for a couple of years, and Saudi before that. Now that's a place to avoid. Nothin' but sand. But I made a helluva lot of cash there. That kept me goin' for a while. And then I moved to Belgium. Had me a nice woman who was from Denmark, and we lived in Brussels for a while. But itchy feet brought me to this part of the world. In fact, I own a company out here. We build swimming pools. I make enough so I can ride my bike whenever I want, except for when I pull stupid stunts."

He took another gulp of beer and laughed. "A few months back, I decided to pull the front wheel of my bike off the ground. I know it's a stupid thing to do, but sometimes, you've gotta have a blast. I thought it'd be cool to do it all the way down the main street, right outside where we're sitting now. Anyhow, I came off and broke my collarbone. I ended up in Bangkok for a titanium plate. Maybe it's time I grew up."

We talked about places we'd been, and places we'd love to go in future. I mentioned the Philippines, because Angela and I were going there later in our trip.

Chuck nodded. "I love that country. Been there many times. The Filipinos are – how can I put it – very accommodating."

While I ordered another beer, he elaborated. "Look, I'm not married, don't want to be. So when I go to places like Bangkok or Manila, I become a sex tourist. There's no shame in that. I like a lady's company, and am prepared to pay for it."

After that bombshell, our conversation drifted onto less controversial topics. "I just bought a silk tie," I told Chuck, "from the night market down the road. I paid three dollars. You've lived here a while, so was that a bargain or have I been ripped off?"

Chuck laughed. "Well, let's put it this way. When I worked in the corporate world, I'd think nothing of paying a hundred dollars for a silk tie. You paid three, so it's all relative. If you think you got a bargain, you did, end of story."

When it was time to leave, I shook Chuck's hand. He was obviously an intelligent man, and I was glad I'd met him. He was witty, charming and, above all else, real. Plus, I'd never met a sex tourist before. I walked across the road to meet Angela so we could get something to eat.

3

The main streets of downtown Siem Reap were full of establishments catering for tourists. Backpacker hostels, tourist information, laundry shops, hot-air-balloon booking centres and Lucky Burger cafes (the Cambodian version of McDonald's) lined the streets.

We decided to eat at a restaurant called Dead Fish. Despite its unappealing name, it turned out to be okay. The food was tasty and cheap, and the Angkor Beer cooling. Across from us sat a group of young backpackers. Instead of sitting at tables and chairs, they had elected to sit cross-legged on the floor, thereby gaining what they hoped was the full authentic eating experience.

We'd seen plenty of young people in town already – most of them from the UK and Ireland, but occasionally from Australia. In fact, earlier that afternoon, we'd witnessed an Australian tourist do something horrible.

Angela and I had been sitting in an outdoor bar when four young Australian men came and sat at the next table. They were all tanned and loud, and one of them had shoulder-length blonde hair – the archetypal surfer dude. All of them ordered a beer and began to laugh and joke with each other.

A small, elderly Cambodian woman walked up to them. She was carrying a large tray of cooked spiders in her hand. Each one was about as big as my fist. They looked like they had been deep-fried.

"Hey," one of the Aussie boys said. "I dare you to eat one!" He was speaking to the blonde man.

"Yeah," another added.

The surfer dude handed the woman a dollar and she passed him a dark brown spider from the top of the pile. The woman then walked off, her tray of goodies balanced carefully on her upturned hand.

Angela and I watched while Surfer Boy and his friends regarded the dead spider. One of them declared it gross, which made the others laugh. Unfazed by the sight of a deep fried spider in his hand, the blonde man snapped off one of the spider's legs. His friends erupted into raucous laughter. He sniffed it and then bit off one end. His pals laughed even more.

"Not bad," Surfer Boy announced, munching away. "It's like a potato chip." He ate the rest of the leg and then snapped off another. He offered it to his friends but they all waved it away, so he ate it himself and then happily munched on the remaining legs.

His friends were finding the whole episode amusing, but mixed with the frivolity was an undercurrent of horror. I could see it on their faces, and on Angela's too. Only the spider's body now remained. It looked hideous and unnatural. I was hoping Surfer Boy was going to discard it.

He didn't.

Raising what remained of the fried arachnid to his mouth, he let it linger there, as if considering what he was about to do. His three friends stopped laughing and began to grimace. Then he bit into it, and what happened next was truly disgusting: a sight I will never forget. From the body, an ungodly grey bile erupted. The mess spilled out over the young man's chin and onto his lap. It was revolting.

"No way...," one of his friends said, as horrified as the rest of us. "There are eggs in it."

"Jesus," said another.

Even Surf Boy looked disturbed. He threw the remainder of the spider's body onto the floor and wiped his mouth, spitting out the horrible mess.

"I can't eat that," he said quietly, staring at the mess he'd created. "That's too much, man."

4

The next day was our big sightseeing extravaganza. Angkor (the place, as opposed to the temple) had once been the ancient capital of the Khmer Empire, with a territory extending across much of modern-day Cambodia, Laos and Thailand. Angkor Wat was the grandest temple they built, and as such, became a symbol of Cambodia, featuring on its currency and flag.

Our guide, a thin young man called Nonin, met us in the hotel lobby and took us out to the car and driver. A few minutes later, we set off. Like in Hanoi, small, thin motorbikes ruled the roads of Siem Reap, though thankfully not in the same concentration as the Vietnamese capital. As we approached the outskirts of town, we passed a large children's hospital. A sign by its entrance read: *Severe Epidemic of Dengue Fever*. The hospital was appealing for people to give blood.

"Angkor Wat is the largest religious monument in the world," said Nonin, as we threaded our way along a road cutting through dense foliage. "And it was constructed in the 12th century. But we will begin the tour in Angkor Thom, the ancient capital city of the Khmer Empire. It is about two kilometres north of Angkor Wat. In its time, a crocodile-infested moat surrounded Angkor Thom. But the crocodiles have gone."

"Does Cambodia have crocodiles?" asked Angela, as we passed an elephant carrying a couple of western tourists. Both looked like they would have preferred to walk.

"Yes, madam," Nonin replied. "We have crocodiles, but very rare. The only time you will see them are in farms."

Before we had a chance to question him further on this, we came to a busy parking area. The place was full of taxis, cars, tour buses and mini-vans. From what we could gather, every tourist in Cambodia had decided to see Angkor Thom at the same time as us.

5

All around us, people were nudging for position on the sandstone blocks that formed the entrance of the walled Angkor Thom. Ruins were everywhere, including huge smiling faces carved into the rocks and walls. Most of the tourists seemed to be from Japan, Korea or China, and the noise they were creating was a constant hum of conversation and sounds of awe. But the number of guides was equally as staggering. Nonin squeezed between two of them and turned to face us.

"These bas-reliefs," he said, pointing at the intricate engravings on a temple wall, "tell the story of a battle between an ancient king and a demon."

Nodding respectfully, we eyed the patterns, noticing pictures we'd have otherwise missed. Skilful artists had carved scenes of war into the rock face. Others scenes depicted bare-breasted women dancing, or monsters cavorting in hellish pleasure. Unsurprisingly, elephants featured heavily too.

We moved on to a different section, where Nonin gave us another detailed description of every indentation and carving. My mind started to wander. I couldn't help it, and when we stopped at the third, fourth and fifth section of wall, I grew bored. Even descriptions of great feasting, visions of hell or people being eaten by crocodiles couldn't maintain my interest.

Because of the concentration of tourists, there were plenty of touts in force. Most were trying to sell water or postcards, but some were dressed up in traditional Khmer costume, ready to pose with tourists willing to part with a little cash. Even though it was highly tacky, we gave them a dollar and posed. The resulting photo was actually quite good.

"Okay, now we go to the famous temple," Nonin said, perhaps sensing my unrest. We got back into the car for the brief journey to Angkor Wat, the air conditioning a welcome respite from the overwhelming heat outside.

Ten minutes later, Nonin was leading us across a wide bridge that spanned a lake. On a nearby wall sat a saffron-robed monk speaking into his phone. A few children were sitting at the edge of the water with fishing nets. At the far end of the bridge stood the walls of the iconic Angkor Wat, its unmistakable towers rising over the tree line. It is always strange seeing something previously only viewed on TV or in books, but there it was in front of us – and it looked magnificent. We stood still for a moment, forgetting about the heat and humidity, ignoring the teenage girls trying to sell us bangles, and simply gazed at the jungle-covered temple.

Our guide led us to a small lily pond. "Good for photo," he said, as he angled us into position. When he showed us the resulting image, it looked great. It looked as if Angela and I were standing in front of a huge lake and not just a tiny pond. We thanked him and wandered to a nearby market stall. Local children tried to sell us postcards and bottles of water, and, after buying some water, we headed for the temple entrance. The chirping call of tropical insects trumpeted our every step.

6

"Okay, this bas relief is on three levels," said Nonin. Angela looked interested, but I was dismayed at the number of carvings on offer. I calculated that Nonin would take an hour to describe them all. And the fact I was bored upset me too. Here I was, at one of the prime attractions of the world, and I couldn't even bring myself to enjoy the vivid descriptions behind its history. I was like a little boy forced to do homework.

With real effort, I tuned back into Nonin's voice. We had moved a few feet along the wall. "This top layer shows heaven, the middle layer depicts normal, everyday life, and the bottom layer shows Hell. Look at this man here." The engraving depicted a man being stabbed in the eye with a red-hot poker. Okay, I thought, that was fairly interesting. Another carving showed a woman being tortured.

Someone had stuck six-inch nails into every part of her body. After a few moments, Nonin moved on, and I couldn't help stifle a yawn. Angela stamped on my foot.

"Monkeys!" I announced. "Over there!" Our guide paused in his monologue and looked over. He decided to cut short his lesson on ancient Khmer history and led us to the animals instead.

The monkeys were great. There was a whole troop of them. As well as entertaining us, they were delighting a family of Japanese tourists who'd also spotted them. One little boy giggled as a monkey stole some sweets from him. The tiny primate ran on all fours and stopped a short distance away. Cool as a cucumber, it started to lick and chew its new sugary treat.

7

For lunch, Nonin took us to a nearby cafe. Every patron was a tourist. The guides seemed to know each other because they were all sitting at the same tables at the back. Nonin joined them, saying he would collect us in forty minutes.

Just beyond the boundary of the cafe were some street children selling bangles and postcards. We called over one boy, aged about eight, and bought some pictures of Angkor Wat from him. Soon other children began to materialise. "What about me!" they wailed. "What about me? I hungry! Please give dollar!"

For the afternoon segment of our tour, Nonin drove us to a floating village. It was about thirty minutes south of Siem Reap. As we reached the outskirts of town, the new hotels disappeared and were replaced by wooden shacks. Despite their appearance, Nonin told us they belonged to rich people because they had electricity. Five minutes later, these houses made way for tiny shacks with corrugated metal roofs. These had no electricity. Most of them had stalls at the front selling fruit and vegetables. People slept in hammocks near them.

Every now and again, we would pass a busy workshop. Piles of motorbike and car engine parts filled each forecourt, with old motorbikes taking up most of the work. Nothing was wasted in Cambodia, we were quickly discovering. If it had once worked, then it would again.

"Floating village not far," said Nonin.

8

The road turned into a causeway. On both sides of us was water filled with 'floating' houses. Most of them were standing on wooden stilts above the swell of the river. Others had simply been converted from boats. The scene looked medieval and *poor*.

Our driver parked the car. "We take boat now," said Nonin. "You will see some of these homes up close. But please remember, the people who live in them are very poor. If you can spare any money and buy a few things, they will be most grateful."

As well as the houses, there was also a floating school, church, and even a floating supermarket. Naked children jumped from tiny makeshift piers, and, further along, a trio of fisherman were bringing their nets in. Small silver fish spilled out onto the bank. Soon, we were on our way.

Everywhere we looked, something interesting was going on: a woman swinging her baby to sleep in a hammock to our right; a boy rowing about in a small metal tub to our left. And though these people were impossibly poor by our western standards, they all seemed genuinely happy.

Twenty minutes later, we pulled up alongside a long wooden jetty and climbed out. Within seconds, four small children who had just rowed across from a nearby shack accosted us. Three of them held creatures out for us to handle in the hope we'd give them a dollar. The fourth child, the youngest, had nothing except an inquisitive look about him.

Angela held a baby crocodile, while I opted to have a snake draped across my shoulders. A third child, a girl of about six, had a large toad tied to a piece of string. She held it out for me to touch.

"No thanks," I said, but gave her a dollar anyway.

As we turned to walk away, the fourth child cried out. "What about me! Give dollar! Please!" He then started to cry, and, whether real or fake, it had the desired effect: we gave him a dollar. They all went away happy.

"Come," said Nonin. "I show you crocodiles."

We followed him to a large enclosure surrounded by a high fence. Down below, in a pit filled with shallow water, were a dozen or so large crocodiles. They were hardly moving except to yawn or to waddle to a sunnier spot. I asked where the creatures had come from.

"From the south. Farmers catch young crocodile and sell them to farm here. Then it grow big. Crocodile is used for meat, and its skin for shoes and bags."

I looked at Angela quizzically. *Was that legal?* Later, when I checked, I found out that the Siamese crocodile was actually a critically endangered species. But that was in the wild. In farms across Southeast Asia, there were thousands of them.

9

When we got back in the boat, I couldn't help notice the driver's foot. His big toe had a bandage around it, and some of his other toes had angry red welts. The pedal he was using to accelerate the boat was clearly the cause. It was a bit of rusty metal. If the young man was in pain, however, he didn't show it. He deftly manoeuvred his vessel into its parking spot so that we could disembark.

As soon as we arrived back at the hotel, the rains that had been promised for much of the day began in earnest. Suddenly, the bone-dry roads became an orangey-brown river that splashed over pavements and into shop doorways. There was sediment everywhere. That night, while wandering in search of an eatery, we often had to choose whether to wade through deep, dark puddles or walk around them, risking cars running us down. Pavements were not an option, due to the number of vehicles parked on them. We finished the night in a restaurant owned by a Frenchman. Our time in Siem Reap was almost over, and it had been a fantastic time. Next stop was the Cambodian capital, Phnom Penh.

Chapter 5. The Killing Fields of Phnom Penh

It only took forty minutes to fly from Siem Reap to the Cambodian capital. The landing was smooth, and we were soon out of the airport, driving into the hustle and bustle of downtown Phnom Penh.

Outside was hot and dusty, the streets clogged with motorcycles and pedestrians. One small scooter had a family of five squashed onto it, two of the adults holding toddlers in their arms. None of them wore crash helmets. Another motorbike had a cage filled with piglets.

Compared to Siem Reap, Phnom Penh was a major city, but a Third World one. Instead of new hotels and tourists, shoeless children and scrawny dogs wandered the pavements, trying to keep out of the sunlight. The buildings beyond them looked like hovels and shacks.

After being dropped off at the hotel, Angela and I headed outside. The streets were crowded with people, the stench was horrendous and the children hawking bottles of water for a dollar were relentless.

"You want water? Where you from? Ah, England, lubbly-jubbly! You buy water from me? Okay, maybe later? You please remember me!"

"This is the hottest day so far," I said as we wandered towards Wat Phnom, a pagoda just opposite our hotel. "I feel like I'm on a barbecue." The small pagoda stood on top of a small hill populated by monkeys. As we headed up a narrow winding path, we spotted one, and then another and another. They were everywhere, indifferent to all the people around them.

One walked straight towards us. When we stopped, it stopped too, its tiny hands fishing around in the dirt. Eventually, it came across a nut of some kind. When Angela tried to stroke its head, the monkey bared its teeth and growled.

Wat Phnom seemed quite unremarkable, especially after the temples of Angkor. Even though seven-headed serpents and demonic lions lined its steps, and its interior was full to the brim with Buddha statues and lit candles, I think Angela and I were simply *templed out*. After a few minutes, we headed back down monkey hill.

2

"Hello, sir! You want tuk-tuk to Royal Palace? Russian Market?" said a man leaning against his colourful little vehicle. We politely said no. Despite the heat, we wanted to find our own way to the Royal Palace.

We passed through a street that smelled particularly awful. It was the stench of rotting vegetables. Piles of decomposing produce were piled next to overflowing bins that looked like they had not been emptied for months. Every heap was covered in flies, some of the coatings so thick that they looked like black viscous blankets. And nearby, people were sleeping on rough bits of cloth. The scene was of pure squalor.

Crossing a busy road, we headed for the riverside promenade. It was a long stretch of pavement full of flags, palm trees and orange-robed monks holding umbrellas. It was a nicer, more tourist-friendly part of Phnom Penh, especially with a view of the river on our left-hand side. Plus the smell was bearable.

The Tonle Sap River was a wide expanse of brown water favoured by narrow wooden boats. Some small boys were jumping off a small pier into the river. All of them were naked, but clearly loving every minute of their fun. A large tuk-tuk sped by. Six shaven-headed monks were sitting in the back. Some stared as they passed.

As we neared the Royal Palace, we couldn't help but notice the cages filled with tiny chirping birds, which, as in Vientiane, could be set free for a small fee. One cage was empty, except for a tiny dead bird at the bottom. "It's so sad," said Angela. "Why do they do this to those poor creatures?" This time we did not pay to set any free.

As it happened, we couldn't get into the Royal Palace. We'd stupidly forgotten about shoulders having to be covered, and the man in charge waved us away. Cursing ourselves, we climbed into a tuk-tuk and asked the driver to take us to the Russian Market. We'd be able to buy something there.

The journey took us past some other unsightly parts of the Cambodian capital, especially rundown apartment buildings. A lot of them were dirty grey, covered in black smears, with piles of litter around their bases. But at least the sun was out.

The Russian Market was so called because of its popularity with Russian ex-pats during the 1980s. It was a sweatbox of humanity and humidity. Inside its narrow, crowded aisles, the heat was almost unbearable. "Hello sir, madam," we heard as we passed every stall. "Please see my store!" After twenty minutes, we'd had enough, but at least we'd managed to buy some cheap clothing to cover Angela's shoulders.

3

The French had built the Royal Palace in the mid-19th century, when Cambodia had been part of French Indochina. It resembled the Grand Palace complex in Bangkok, we thought, only without the masses of tourists. Instead of hundreds of people, there were perhaps twenty in total, all of them Westerners. We joined them, stepping into the well-manicured grounds, surprised to find out that the current king still resided inside the Royal Palace. The sections where he lived were closed to the public.

Gold glittered from the spiky temple roofs. Monkeys scratched themselves on the palace walls. There was not one fragment of litter anywhere. It was quiet. The complex looked beautiful. "We are looking for something called the Silver Pagoda," I said to

Angela. "It contains the Emerald Buddha." I looked at my map, trying to work out where we were.

"Another emerald Buddha? Why are they always green?" asked Angela. "That one in Bangkok was green too."

"I think green is supposed to mean he's in an enlightened state."

"So you'll never be green then."

We carried on walking through the grounds, passing bushes the palace gardeners had intricately preened and shaped. Scuttling lizards darted from shadows. We stopped so I could get my bearings. The Silver Pagoda was being particularly elusive.

"Why don't we follow that red arrow?" said Angela. "It says the Silver Pagoda is along there."

"Ooh," I said, looking up, "aren't you the enlightened one?"

We soon arrived at another beautiful temple. But it wasn't silver. It was white and red, with a roof of orange, green and gold. After removing our shoes, we entered the Silver Pagoda and found out why it had received its name. It was to do with the floor. Five thousand silver blocks, weighing almost six tonnes, lined the base of the pagoda. Unfortunately, large carpets covered them. We wandered around the building, eyeing the small Emerald Buddha placed high in the centre of the temple, and the much more impressive Maitreya Buddha. It was a life-sized golden effort, its body encrusted with thousands of diamonds.

"Let's go back to the hotel for a swim," I suggested. Sweat was oozing from every pore of my body and I needed respite from it. No wonder so many of the locals were wandering around with umbrellas. We flagged down a tuk-tuk and were soon on our way.

4

The next morning looked hot and humid again. Outside our fifth-floor window, it seemed like steam was rising from the pavements. A tuk-tuk sped past, and then a man pulling a cart filled with rubbish did. Whether he'd collected it, or was about to deposit it, I didn't know.

Suddenly, a pedestrian stepped into the road and a fast-moving tuk-tuk hit him. The man went down and did not get up. The tuk-tuk driver pulled over and climbed out. He bent over the unmoving man, saying something I couldn't hear. Another man rushed over to the scene, and then another. Soon a small crowd had gathered around the man lying in the road.

"Oh my God," said Angela, joining me at the window. "What happened?"

I told her and she shook her head. "Do you think he's okay?"

"I don't know. The tuk-tuk was going pretty fast..."

As we watched the drama, someone lunged and then pushed at the tuk-tuk driver. He staggered backwards but did not fall. He moved away from the crowd, keeping a safe distance. From somewhere, a thick blanket appeared, and the injured man was placed onto it. A group of men lifted and then carried the man away. The crowd dispersed, leaving only the tuk-tuk driver. After a moment of simply staring after them, he inspected the front of his vehicle, and then climbed back in. Off he went, more slowly this time.

Before stepping outside, I told Angela I wanted to buy a headband, the type favoured by tennis players. As well as keeping my eyes free from salty perspiration, it would hopefully make me look stylish and dapper.

"You're not buying a headband," said Angela.

"Why not?"

Angela shot me a look. "Because you'll look like an idiot. Just put your cap on, and keep wiping your face. I'm not walking with you if you buy a tennis headband. Besides, I doubt they'll even sell them here."

We jumped in a tuk-tuk and asked the driver to take us to the Tuol Sleng Genocide Museum, the place where the Khmer Rouge had interrogated and tortured its citizens.

5

The building had once been a high school. It was in the middle of the city, surrounded by dirty streets and spindly palm trees. Inside the entrance, we regarded the three-storey concrete structure. It did look like a school, we both agreed. Even the grassy area in front of it looked like the place where children would have congregated during their breaks. But, of course, when the Khmer Rouge had taken over the country in 1975 (renaming it Kampuchea in the process), schooling had been abolished, and they had used the school field as an area of torture.

Pol Pot, a hard-line communist, had been the leader of the Khmer Rouge. He wanted Kampuchea to be rural and classless, and he sought to do this by banning ownership of anything. He abolished the need for money, outlawed religion, and made everyone wear simple black clothes. In order to stop discussion of his regime, he banned people from leaving their immediate area, and prohibited more than two people meeting at any one time. If a group of three people were caught talking, they were often sent to prison for interrogation and then execution.

S-21 (or Tuol Sleng Prison), the place Angela and I were looking at, became one of the main headquarters of this interrogation and torture.

6

"This is horrible," Angela whispered as we walked around the room. Stark black and white portrait photos of people brought to Security Prison 21 filled it. Men, women and children lined the displays, their mug shots taken on arrival. Most looked terrified, but some were smiling, as if they had no clue about what was in store for them. One large photo showed a woman holding a baby. The expression on her face was neutral.

"Here she is again," said Angela. The second photo of the woman had been taken from the side, and this time the baby was nowhere to be seen. She still had the same neutral expression as before, except for one important detail. Running down her face was a single tear. Angela looked away. "This is so sad."

We found the interrogation cells. We entered one to find yellow, plastered walls, with light coming in from a single window. Five or six bats hung in the corner of the room. The floor was chequered tiles, reminding us again that this terrible place had been a school. In the centre of the room was a single metal-framed bed. The stains underneath suggested some of the horrors administered there. More obvious was the large black and white photo on the wall. It was chilling to even glance at, horrific to linger upon. In fact, we were both thankful we couldn't really make out what had happened to the man.

In another room, an artist's impressions of the atrocities committed managed to put colour to the horror. One painting showed a terrified man with his feet shackled, his forearms encased in some sort of wooden block. His torturer was in the foreground with a pair of pliers. Blood was pooled on the floor, along with the man's fingernails. Angela gasped when she joined me at the gruesome picture. "What were they supposed to admit to?"

"Nothing," I answered. "They couldn't admit to anything because they hadn't done anything. They were just educated people, doctors, teachers, or those who worked for the previous government. But not just them – their families too."

On an upper level of the prison were the cells. Each individual cell was tiny, not even wide enough to stretch my arms out in, but they still would have housed six or seven people. Rules had to be followed inside the cells, even some impossible ones. For instance, if a person moved in their sleep (without first asking for permission), they would be punished with lashes from an electrical cord.

In total, more than 17,000 people were imprisoned in S-21, and only twelve survived the ordeal. One was a man called Vann Nath, a skilled artist. He survived because his paintings of Pol Pot were so good. The horrific paintings we'd just looked at were Nath's work. Another inmate survived because of his great skill at fixing the prison's sewing machines.

We came to a small room holding some sort of exhibition. There were about eight pairs of photos, all former guards at the prison. Each pair of photos showed the same person, then and now. "Look at this one," I said to Angela. The black and white photo showed a boy of fourteen wearing a dark cap. He looked the child he was. The placard underneath said his position was *Combatant*. The colour photo next to it showed a 42-year-old man chopping a piece of wood. It was the same person. He looked like any other Cambodian man we'd seen, certainly not a monster. The next photo showed a man cradling his young daughter.

"You know," I said. "These people are brave to have their pictures put up here. They have normal lives now, and yet they're prepared to admit what they once were."

Suitably saddened by what we had seen inside the prison, we caught another tuk-tuk to the Killing Fields, located 15km away. It was where the Khmer Rouge finally murdered the prisoners after their interrogations.

7

"Hello," the young man said, in remarkably good English. We'd just hired him as our guide. His name was Samnang. "Let's sit for a moment while I tell you about this terrible place."

Samnang led us to some wooden benches offering a bit of shade. The landscape was green and pleasant. We were not in fields as such; it was more a collection of grassy areas surrounded by clumps of trees, bushes and fences. Chickens pecked about in the dirt, and in the distance was the honking of traffic. Our guide began to speak.

"All the prisoners from S-21 were brought here. When they first arrived, they were blindfolded. Guards led them to the fields and killed them straight away. Usually it was with a spade or hatchet because bullets were too expensive. Maybe three hundred people a day were killed like this."

Samnang stared at us. His eyes looked sad. "You may have noticed that Cambodian people don't talk much about this atrocity. But I promise you that we never forget. Every May, Cambodian families bring their children here to see what Pol Pot did. They teach them, so it can never happen again."

Just beyond where Angela and I were sitting was a pagoda filled with skulls: over eight thousand of them, according to Samnang. "This place was like a factory," he told us. "The prisoners were laid out side by side, not allowed to speak, not allowed to move, and then, one by one, their skulls were bashed with a tool. Music blasted from loudspeakers to muffle the wails, and when they were dead, they were thrown into mass graves. I will show you these now. Please come."

We followed Samnang along a dirt path. The narrow trail was littered with fragments of clothing belonging to the victims. The first grave we came to was little more than the size of a garden pond. It was a rough patch of ground with weeds poking out from the soil. A sign read: *Please don't walk through the mass grave.*

Samnang said, "When the Khmer Rouge buried people, they did not do it according to religion or creed. No, bodies were dumped on top of each other without thought. Then they were covered in dirt. But as the bodies decomposed, they filled with gas. This caused some of them to rise to the surface. That is how the graves were eventually found. This single grave here held maybe fifty bodies."

"And this tree trunk," said the guide, leading us to a gnarled tree that would've looked good in any British garden, "was where guards killed babies. They smashed their tiny bodies against the trunk like pieces of rubbish. And then they threw them in here." Samnang pointed to another mass grave in front of us. "This one was full of women and children." Both Angela and I were silent, imagining the horror of it all. "The women were all naked; most of them had been raped by the guards before being killed."

To say the place was harrowing would be an understatement. It was a place of nightmares. And as we followed Samnang past another mass grave, he explained a little more about the Khmer Rouge.

"Pol Pot was pure evil," he said, matter-of-factly. "He wanted to get rid of anyone with an education so he could start from year zero. In his mind, farmers would take over the land, providing everything the country needed. Intellectuals were a barrier to his plan, so they had to be re-educated. This of course meant being killed. For the guards of the Khmer Rouge, they were not killing innocent people, they were only re-educating them."

I looked at Angela. Her facial expression was the same as mine: uncomprehending horror.

"Children were easy to manipulate," he told us. "So the Khmer Rouge used them as guards in S-21. The children knew no difference, only what they were told to believe. So you can't really blame them. In fact, the Khmer Rouge kidnapped a lot of young children. They took them to indoctrination camps."

I thought of the photo exhibition we saw back in the prison. Young guards barely into their teens. Many of them had tortured their own citizens, maybe even people they knew.

"They were told not to show any emotion, any sympathy. They were not allowed to laugh or cry. They were like robots, obeying only the regime. But sometimes even the guards were not safe. Look."

We arrived at another mass grave, this one surrounded by a wooden fence. It had a sign that read: *Mass graves of victims without heads.*

"These were Pol Pot's soldiers and guards," Samnang explained. "Their heads were cut off to make sure they were really dead. But it wasn't just the soldiers who were killed. Their wives and children were slaughtered too. He didn't want any memory of the men to remain."

I asked why the Khmer Rouge would want to kill their own guards.

"Many reasons," Samnang answered. "But it all boiled down to one thing: they thought they were traitors."

We passed a palm tree that had some of its branches cut short. Samnang stopped next to it. "Feel this branch here," he said. Both Angela and I did so, feeling the rough, serrated edge.

"It was where guards cut prisoners' throats. The edge was sharp enough to do this."

8

At the entrance to the skull pagoda was a long length of shackles. Samnang noticed me staring. "The guards told prisoners to lie down on their front with their eyes shut. These shackles went around their ankles. An iron bar was pushed through a gap to hold all the prisoners in place. Maybe twelve prisoners were connected in this way."

I looked closer. Each shackle had a small circular hole that an iron bar could be fed along. The guide explained further. "As you would expect, some prisoners had bigger feet than others, but this did not matter to the guards. They would bang the metal rod through, breaking ankle bones so it went to the next shackle."

The pagoda was full of human skulls, pile upon pile of them, shelf upon shelf. Some had bullet holes, but most were simply caved in. We walked past the displays in silence, shocked and incredibly saddened by the sight of them all. The Killing Fields had been in operation for three years, until Vietnam invaded Kampuchea in 1979, and the Khmer Rouge regime crumbled. But during those three terrible years, due to a mixture of executions, starvation and poor medical care, between one and three million people died. That was a quarter of the population.

Angela and I arrived back at our hotel, suitably humbled. And to think that Pol Pot had only died in 1998 (from malaria), without having to face any charges of mass genocide against his own people. Unbelievable.

9

"You want boat ride?" asked a thin, wiry man sitting on a plastic chair along Sisowath Quay, the main artery along the river. Unlike most of the other boat touts we'd passed, this man didn't seem part of an official company. In fact, as far as we could tell, he didn't have a boat. We stopped to face him. A boat ride was exactly what we needed. It had been a few hours since the Killing Fields, and we desperately needed some breeze to lighten our sweat-laden brows.

"How much?" I asked.

"Sixteen dollar!" he said without pause. "For one hour!"

I looked at Angela. Ten dollars was the maximum we'd budgeted for a short trip along the Tonle Sap River. It had no sights as such, and all we wanted was to relax from the deck of a boat. I turned to the man and shook my head. "Too much!" I said. "Ten dollars."

The man smiled, shaking his head back at me. He looked about forty, but was probably much younger. "Okay," he said. "Twelve dollar."

Again, I shook my head, and led Angela away, but the man soon stopped us. "Okay, yes, ten dollar. Come."

We followed the man towards a mooring point, delighted to find that he did indeed have a boat. It was parked next to another boat. Both of them looked old. He took us across a wooden plank to the empty vessel, and then ushered us towards the rear. Then he left us. Perhaps he'd gone to drum up more trade for the tour.

We decided to make ourselves at home, and found some plastic seats. Pot plants were everywhere, and cobwebs littered the masts and tables. The ropes tying us to the embankment looked like they had been in place for years.

"This boat hasn't been out in while," I said to Angela. She nodded, applying a bit of sun-tan spray. Just then, the man returned with his wife and young daughter in tow. The girl was aged about six. While we waited for the tour to begin, the adults rushed hither and thither getting the vessel shipshape. The girl cleaned a few things too, and, a few minutes later, we heard the starter motor turn over. Then it went quiet again.

I raised my eyebrows to Angela. A commotion started below deck. After a moment, the woman wandered past us smiling sweetly. She was carrying a machete. Once more, we heard the engine turn over. This time it produced a belch of black smoke. Then it died again.

Just then, we caught sight of some activity from the boat next door. A teenage boy was carrying a large battery, the sort of device that could hopefully kick-start our boat's engine into life. Our man jumped across to help him, and when he caught our gaze, he bowed and apologized. "Five minutes," he promised. They disappeared below deck.

A few minutes later, the engine was cranked for a third time, and this time it spluttered into some sort of belated life. It didn't live long though, because, after five seconds, the boat became silent once more. The death throes, I felt.

By now, a small crowd had gathered on the bank. Four children from the boat next door were also watching with interest and then, high up on the embankment, a security guard appeared. He seemed to be laughing.

"Shall we get off?" I shouted up at him.

The man laughed, and then nodded.

The wife wandered past again. She still had the machete, but also had a fistful of electrical cables. As she passed us, she smiled and apologized again. And then we heard a splash. We turned just in time to see her husband disappear into the water. Every now and again, he'd pop up for air before diving back down again. Maybe the propeller was covered in seaweed or something.

"I hope he gets it going," said Angela. "We're probably his first paying passengers for months. And this boat is their home. They're all his neighbours." She waved at the boys on the boat next door; they waved back. I waved at the small crowd on the bank and they all waved back too.

"How about this," Angela said. "Even if he doesn't get it going, we should still give him a few dollars. I feel so sorry for them."

I nodded in agreement.

Time passed, and both of us were feeling very self-conscious. There were now about ten people on the riverbank, and some of them had sat down to watch the show. Another onlooker joined the security guard and said something. They both laughed uproariously.

To pass the time, we gave the small boys on the next boat some Cambodian riels, about twenty-five pence worth. They took the wad of almost worthless banknotes and grinned. And then the husband splashed noisily aboard the boat. "We go now!" he announced proudly.

And he was right. Somehow, he coaxed the ancient engine from the dead, and we were soon off, heading at a fair clip across the river. Our audience clapped and cheered.

10

From the deck of the oldest sailing boat in town, Angela and I enjoyed some of the other sights of Phnom Penh. Across the other side of the river was a collection of shacks. Behind them were some grander-looking buildings, fenced off from the hovels. A fisherman with a simple hook and line was sitting in a small wooden boat moored in the middle of the river. Judging by the belongings crammed inside a tiny roofed section, it was his home.

"If we sink," I said, peering around the boat for safety equipment, "don't except to be rescued. We'll have to swim for it. At least there doesn't seem to be any crocodiles."

An hour later, we were safely moored back where we started. As we left, we paid the man an extra couple of dollars and thanked him. He bowed in return, as did his wife. Their daughter was curled up asleep on a hammock. We climbed back up the embankment, happy and strangely content.

11

That evening, Angela and I caught a tuk-tuk to a restaurant recommended by our guidebook. It described the food as being exquisite. Exquisite was not the word we would have chosen.

The Pyongyang Restaurant was part of a chain of establishments owned by the North Korean government. As well as serving strange food on its menu, there was also the promise of karaoke.

The place was half-full of oriental men, who the guidebook suggested would be South Koreans. The waitresses were all young and attractive, wearing exactly the same light blue uniform, with their hair tied back severely. They looked identical. All of them were North Koreans. Photography was banned inside the restaurant but, as we took our seats, I managed to sneak off a quick photo while pretending to put the camera on the floor.

"Why did we come here?" asked Angela, reading the menu. It offered things such as Pig Intestines and something delicious called Mashed Pork Paw. The glare from the overhead lights was reflecting off the menu. Ambient lighting was not a concern for the hospital-ward-lit Pyongyang Restaurant.

"I don't know." My eyes lingered on a dish called Seasoned Cow Stomach, and then on something called Dog Soup. Eventually, I opted for something called Fish with Vegetable Sauce. Angela went for the simple sounding Duck.

My food was hideous; the grey-fleshed fish still had all its skin on, with the head being particularly gruesome. Two eyes peered up at me, covered in some sort of batter, and, as I prodded it, some dark stuff seeped out from beneath the skull. However, no matter how bad mine was, Angela's was worse.

Her duck was 95% fat and skin. The pimpled skin where the feathers had been plucked was clearly visible. It wouldn't have surprised me to find a bit of beak or even a webbed foot in there somewhere. Angela grimly picked up a piece of duck gristle and studied it for a moment before popping it into her mouth. I almost gagged. I picked at my fish while Angela sucked on the fat, trying to extract any meat that might be there.

"Well, this is nice," I quipped.

After a softly spoken waitress had cleared our almost untouched plates away, we wondered whether to stay for the entertainment. According to what we'd read, at 8pm sharp some of the waitresses changed clothes and then danced for the audience; others played musical instruments and sang. It was all a precursor to the karaoke

"I think we should go before it starts," said Angela. "Besides, we need to find somewhere else to eat. I'm still hungry."

Ten minutes later, we were back in a tuk-tuk, heading to a restaurant near our hotel. Our last night in Phnom Penh was almost over.

Chapter 6. Beach Time in Phuket

Thailand's largest island had once been a major trading point between India and China. In its day, many of Phuket's citizens had grown rich from the export of tin and rubber. Nowadays, of course, tourism is Phuket's main source of income, and, for Angela and me, it was to be our first beach stop of Southeast Asia. After travelling through Laos, Vietnam and Cambodia, the lure of a nice hotel with its own private beach was simply irresistible.

Touching down at Phuket International, the sun was shining, the sky was blue, and our mood was good. We collected our luggage and stepped out to hail a taxi.

"This is nicer than Phnom Penh," I said, as we sped away from the terminal. The road looked clean, the cars in better shape, and even the jungle on both sides looked thick and healthy.

"Yeah," agreed Angela. "I'm looking forward to doing nothing for a few days."

2

Our hotel was on the south-eastern tip of Phuket, a forty-minute taxi ride from the airport. When we arrived, we were not disappointed; it was exactly the sort of hotel we'd been hoping for. It even had a balcony overlooking the Andaman Sea. We headed straight for the beach.

It was glorious. The white sand and turquoise water looked truly beautiful and exquisitely tropical. Grabbing a mask and snorkel, we were soon in the sea, wondering what we'd find. The answer turned out to be not that much. Though there were some unidentifiable shapes lurking on the bottom, upon closer inspection, they turned out to be leaves deposited from the nearby palms.

For the next couple of hours, we lounged on the beach reading, and listening to our iPods. At one point, we hired a canoe and went for a quick jaunt around the bay. What a life! How lucky to be able to do what we were doing. And then we returned to the beach to sunbathe under a warm tropical sun, listening as waves gently lapped against the sand. It was only back at the hotel that I realised my folly.

3

My legs were red raw. They looked like slabs of meat. I was lying on the bed staring at them. The area below my swimming shorts formed a distinct border: white, then pure red.

"Jesus," said Angela, staring down at my quivering limbs.

"I know. They're stinging like mad! In fact, I think I might need to go to hospital. What if they're second-degree burns or something? Help me! I'm a lobster."

I'd been so careful up until now. But I had been lulled. Lulled by the fact that I'd been out in the sun for over two weeks without any sunburn whatsoever. But just one afternoon in Phuket had seen it all go horribly wrong.

Angela produced a bottle of aloe vera from her suitcase, instructing me to rub it on gently. I gingerly did so, but the moment the cream touched my legs, it began crackling and hissing. My legs were actually cooking!

We pondered why I'd burnt quite so badly. After all, Angela was fine, even though she'd been out in the sun just as long as I had. After a quick search on the Internet, we found the culprit – my malaria tablets. In an effort to save money, I'd gone for the cheapest brand possible. Angela had refused to get the same ones as me. Hers were more than three times as expensive.

Reading the information leaflet for my tablets, I spotted the warning in bold black lettering: *Avoid direct exposure to the sun, e.g. sunbathing on a sun lounger.* Angela's tablets had no such warning.

"What sort of imbecile invents malaria tablets where you need to avoid exposure to the sun?" I screeched. "It's always hot places where you find mosquitoes. It's like buying a ski jacket with a warning not to wear it in the snow. Idiots."

A few hours later, I attempted to stand up. I felt like a pensioner with arthritis. Getting my jeans on was fun. It felt like my skin was being sheared off, layer by painful layer. Walking was also a novel experience. Moving like a robot without knee joints made Angela laugh. But at least I was mobile. With Angela helping me along, I hobbled towards the hotel's exit. We needed something to eat.

4

The restaurant we chose was just up the hill from our hotel. Luckily, a hotel shuttle bus drove us there, stopping long enough for me to waddle down the steps. The waiter led us to a table that was on a balcony overlooking the sea. The table offered enough room for me to stretch my legs out fully. At half past six, the sun began to set, and, ten minutes later, the insects began their sunset call.

"Here's to Phuket," I said, raising my bottle of Beer Chang. Angela clinked her glass of wine to it.

The meal was great, and, later that night, we were delighted to find a tiny gecko in our room. It was hanging on the wall, hoping to catch stray insects. I went to sleep with my legs wobbling and stinging every time I moved. It was a fitful night, made worse when I discovered the bed sheet was stuck to my aloe vera legs. Getting free of my new skin graft was like pulling the plaster off a not-quite-healed wound.

5

The next morning, the crimson glow had receded a little. I could also move about a little more easily. I even managed to walk down to breakfast unaided.

"That tall man over there has just been really horrible to a waitress," Angela told me.

I looked over to where my wife was pointing. A large Western man was sitting with his wife. They were with another couple. Judging by their accents, they were German. The big man was saying something to his companions. They nodded at something he said.

"I don't know what he said," Angela told me, "but he was towering over her like a giant."

"Which waitress was it?" I asked.

"That poor girl over there: her, by the juice stand."

She looked about eighteen and was tiny, as all of the Thai waitresses were. She looked upset. I stared back at the man. He was clearly still angry about something, muttering to the others. His wife was trying to calm him, but, just then, the man stood up and stomped back to the waitress. He stood over the terrified girl, bringing his face only inches from hers. He was nearly twice her size.

"Let me give you some advice," he bellowed in her face. This was a man clearly not bothered by social etiquette. Everyone in the breakfast hall was watching him. The girl stared up at him, hands raised in self-defence. "Do not approach guests and say: 'napkin'. No! You say: 'Good morning, *sir*. Here is your napkin.' I have paid a lot of money to stay at this hotel and I demand to be treated with respect!"

He stormed off back to his table. His companions looked embarrassed.

The waitress stood still a moment, obviously at a loss, and then promptly burst into tears. Some of her colleagues surrounded her. A few moments later, they led her into a side room.

"What a bully," said Angela. "Who does he think he is? Treat with respect? He needs a lesson in respect."

We left breakfast with a bitter taste in our mouths.

6

Later that evening, bored with the beach, we decided to visit Phuket City. Once again, we availed ourselves of the hotel shuttle bus. Along the way, we passed numerous beauty salons and traditional massage parlours.

Phuket City was a grubby little town, mainly full of gaudy clothes and trinket shops, together with endless stalls selling pirated DVDs. Chinatown was slightly better, heralded by a fine red and orange gateway. But it was still not enough to make us want to linger.

"Let's find somewhere to eat," I said to Angela. "We can either try a restaurant here or go somewhere else."

"Somewhere else," Angela said.

We found a shaded spot and looked in the guidebook for recommendations. "This one sounds all right," said Angela. She showed me the page. "It's near our hotel." I read the description. It sounded fine to me. We flagged down a taxi and told the driver the name of the restaurant.

"I know the one you mean," he said, as we pulled into the honking traffic of downtown Phuket City. "It is very nice. But I know somewhere better – a fish restaurant near it. Local people own it. The other one is owned by Westerners who don't even live in Phuket. Both serve good food, but only one will contribute to the local economy. It is up to you."

We, of course, chose the fish restaurant.

The restaurant was situated near the shore of the Andaman Sea, and, even though it was dark, the sound of the waves made it a good choice for an evening meal. Our food arrived on a fish-shaped metal plate balanced on an open stove. And it was the whole fish: head, tail, bones and all. It was a tasty but messy meal, and, as we tucked in, a young girl approached our table. She had some knickknacks in a bag, and a sign that read: *I am dumb. Please buy from me.*

We did.

"I'm glad we came here," said Angela a few moments later. "It's nice."

Not long after, we returned to the hotel. Our batteries were recharging.

7

The next day, our final day in Phuket, was also my birthday. A cake arrived in our room, courtesy of the hotel management. It was a nice touch to an already fabulous stay. With my legs healing nicely, we headed back to the beach, but this time armed with bread. We wanted to feed the fish.

The previous day we had seen an American couple feeding them. As we'd lain on our sun beds, the thirty-something man and woman had waded into the sea with rolls of bread in their hands. After throwing bits into the clear blue water, a sizeable number of fish arrived, eager for food. We decided we would do the same thing, and had raided the breakfast bar in preparation.

Angela and I entered the Andaman Sea. There didn't seem to be any fish anywhere. Even so, Angela threw a small chunk of bread into the water and, almost immediately, a shoal of fish arrived. They were darting back and forth. We threw more bread in, and were soon surrounded by perhaps a hundred fish, all silvery and inquisitive. Occasionally, we'd catch glimpses of strange translucent fish. They were long and thin, shimmering with fabulous shades of blue and green. Unlike the silver fish, they were shy creatures, keeping their distance and disappearing from sight whenever the other fish approached. Feeding the fish turned out to be a real highlight of our stay in Phuket.

Just along from the beach was a jetty owned by the hotel. It was used as a pick-up point for privately-run boat trips. We walked along the beach, and then made our way along the jetty until we got to the end. Sitting on a ledge underneath was a local fisherman.

His line was submerged into the crystal clear water. By his side were a couple of large fish.

We said hello and he returned the greeting. Just then, there was movement in the water. The man jumped up. "Sea snake!" he said. "Very bad!"

We watched as it swam around at the edge of the jetty before disappearing again. I turned to Angela. We had been snorkelling not far from here earlier. Imagine if a deadly snake had bitten us!

"Come on," I said to Angela. "Time to pack." The second segment of our journey across the Far East was about to begin.

Chapter 7. Hong Kong Phooey

On the flight from Phuket to Hong Kong, I couldn't get a certain song out of my head. It was from a cartoon I used to watch as a kid. *Hong Kong Phooey, number one super guy. Hong Kong Phooey, quicker than the human eye.* The song played over and over in my mind as we flew northwards, until it suddenly occurred to me that perhaps someone aboard the flight was called Phooey. Imagine that, a real life Hong Kong Phooey.

Since 1999, Hong Kong and Macau have been Special Administrative Regions (SAR) of China. This means that, although they are under the overall authority of mainland China, they are more or less autonomous states. They sort out their own affairs and have their own political systems. Their citizens possess Hong Kong or Macau passports instead of Chinese ones, and they use their own currencies to buy things. But the best thing for Angela and me was that, instead of needing a visa to enter Hong Kong (like in mainland China), passport control was a cinch. After clearing customs, we were soon in a car heading to our hotel.

2

The Park Lane Hotel was located in Causeway Bay on Hong Kong Island. Causeway Bay was a skyscraper-heavy part of Hong Kong, possessing the most expensive shopping streets in the world. Our room had a fine view of Victoria Bay and Kowloon beyond. The number of skyscrapers was staggering, as was the lush greenery around them. It was like a tropical New York.

We took a walk around the immediate vicinity, and Angela was delighted to find it was full of modern shops. The tuk-tuks had gone, replaced instead by buses and taxis. People were everywhere, storming into subway stations, rushing along streets, sidestepping slower pedestrians or crowding together as they crossed over busy roads. Gawky teenage boys stood around with their outlandish hairstyles and iPhones. Teenage girls, most of them stick-thin, paraded past in skimpy clothing. Men in suits jostled for position with old Chinese women. Hong Kong was a city of contrasts.

The heat was intense, the sort of temperature you get after opening an oven door, and this made the car fumes noxious. At times, especially when walking between buildings, it felt like we were drowning in hot air. Nevertheless, we wandered around busy streets full of Chinese lettering, marvelling at simply being in Hong Kong.

3

As night fell, the dazzling lights came on across the city. Angela and I caught a tube to Temple Street Night Market in Kowloon, and, as we climbed out of the underground, I couldn't help but feel we'd arrived in the Hong Kong I'd seen on television. Glittering neon signs written in red Chinese lettering hung over the streets and chophouses. The air was thick with exotic conversation and the smell of cooked food. As we got closer to the night market, the crowds thickened.

"I'm hungry," I said, as we hit the first stalls. "I think we should get something to eat first." I spotted a large outdoor eatery called Temple Street Spicy Crabs, and thought it would suffice, especially as it proudly boasted it offered *the real taste of China*. The place was packed, everyone fighting for space at the large white plastic tables. A couple of nerdy oriental men with square black glasses sat chewing on something from their plate. Further along, a whole family was sitting around a table sharing a meal of shrimp and crab.

"Wat yu won?" barked a hard-faced waitress as soon as we'd sat down. It took us a while to work out what she'd said; when we did, we ordered some drinks and something called Chicken in Black

Bean. The waitress nodded and disappeared, reappearing a minute later to plonk down our drinks.

"Service with a smile," Angela said.

Our meals arrived a few minutes later, and we both looked inside the bowls. They contained green peppers, black beans, and chicken parts that should've been thrown away.

"It's pure gristle," said Angela as she picked up a piece with her chopsticks. I looked at my meal and shuddered. It was almost as bad as the Pyongyang Restaurant in Phnom Penh. In the end, of the twenty or so pieces of gizzard in my bowl, I managed to extract perhaps one mouthful of edible meat. The rest I had to discard, including, I'm sickened to say, a ball and socket joint. If this was what the real taste of China was like, then it was something I would try to avoid in the future.

Temple Street Market was smaller than expected, composed of just two main aisles. But it was heaving. It sold the usual assortment of stuff, ranging from knock-off watches, hair clips, paintings, leather bags and fake designer clothes to porno DVDs. Tourists were buying everything with gusto because the prices were dirt-cheap. We wandered from one end to the other, and along the way picked up a few bargains ourselves.

"That's it for souvenirs," I said as we headed away from the market. "Otherwise we'll need another suitcase."

"Don't worry," said Angela. "We've still got plenty of room. Besides, we can always make more room by throwing away some of your clothes and shoes."

I laughed. "I've only got two pairs of shoes! And I'm wearing one pair right now. How many have you got?"

"Two or three..."

"More like seven or eight. The wardrobe in the hotel is packed with your shoes. I might throw some in the harbour."

We made our way back to the hotel. Angela promised she would rein in the spending from now on.

4

The next morning was overcast; the gunmetal-coloured low-level clouds skirted the tops of the skyscrapers. With some drizzle in the air, we headed towards a metro stop so that we could catch a train to the famous Peak Tram.

As we descended the escalators into Hong Kong's subterranean world, we couldn't help but be impressed. Everything was so clean and tidy: not a scrap of litter anywhere. The shops and cafes gave the whole subway the look of an upscale shopping mall.

"Have you noticed the doors?" asked Angela as we took our seats in one of the air-conditioned tube carriages. The automatic doors of the train were closing, but behind them, on the platform, some outer plastic screens were also closing.

I nodded. "I wonder if they're there to stop people committing suicide?"

"Probably."

Half an hour later, we were sitting inside a carriage of the Peak Tram, reputedly the world's steepest funicular railway. As it set off on its upwards trajectory, Angela and I hypothesized on the best way to save ourselves should the cable snap.

"I'd jump out of the window," I said, looking at the scenery we were passing. It was mainly bushes and trees.

Angela shook her head. "I'd curl up behind that bulkhead."

I looked at where she meant and conceded that it might do a decent job. "Not bad, but I still reckon I'd be better off jumping."

"Yeah, but you might roll down the hill, or mistime your jump. You could end up under the wheels."

"Maybe we shouldn't be even talking about this," I suggested.

When we got to the top eight minutes later, the view was incredible, offering a panoramic view of Hong Kong and its harbour. Skyscrapers were on both sides of the inlet, and most of them looked modern and silver.

"Look!" said Angela, pointing into the sky.

An eagle was effortlessly riding the thermals around the lush green mountainside, unaware it was flying above some of the best skyscrapers in the world. With a twist of its tail, it disappeared from view.

In a Peak Tower shop (there was a shopping centre in the complex), we succumbed to another tourist temptation, and bought a handwritten (I actually saw the man doing it) framed picture, with our names written in beautiful Mandarin script.

"This could say anything, though," I said, as we admired the finished product. "In fact it probably says 'tight-arse English bastards'." I was referring to the fact I'd haggled the woman down on her initial asking price, even quibbling over fifty pence.

"Where next?" Angela asked, as we waited for the tram to take us down to street level.

"Ngong Ping 360," I answered.

"What's that?"

"You'll see."

5

Ngong Ping 360 was Hong Kong's cable car system, even though it sounded like some sort of robot to me. It was near the airport, but, with such an efficient tube service, we were there in no time at all.

"Yu won kisstal cabin or nommal?" asked the woman behind the counter. After some consideration, we chose the significantly cheaper normal carriage. The crystal cabin, we later learned, was identical to the normal ones, except for a section of floor made from clear glass. We joined the queue with everybody else and waited.

I detested queuing, and so did Angela, but she didn't hate it as much as me. I'd once thrown a sandwich across the entire length of a supermarket after suffering from a particularly bad incident of queue rage. And in another, I'd actually written a letter of complaint and sent it to the bank while I was standing in their queue.

"Calm down," said Angela, after I'd complained for the third time. It didn't help that the cable car loading station still had about ten thousand people to go. And what really irked me was when some of the cars left empty. What was that about?

Eventually, we made it into one and I calmed down. And as it happened, the twenty-five minute ride up to Ngong Ping Village was just about worth the wait. As we traversed green hills and skyscraper forests, we could see virtually the whole of Hong Kong. Even the airport looked like a toy one: its tiny planes taking off and landing hundreds of feet below us. It was the sort of view the eagle had probably seen over the Peak earlier.

Despite its name, Ngong Ping Village was actually an entertainment centre full of overpriced restaurants and shops. But it did have a huge bronze statue of Buddha nearby. Because of the statue's size, it was known as the Big Buddha, and it towered over one hillside. Angela and I decided not to climb the steps up to it, and found a bar instead. We watched as families wandered past, some of them almost tripping up as they stared upwards at the giant statue.

6

As night fell, Angela and I arrived at the harbour to catch a Star Ferry across to Kowloon. As we made the quick crossing, we couldn't help but marvel at the night-time skyline of Hong Kong, a true wonder of modern times. Some of the skyscrapers looked like they were putting on light shows: multicoloured neon was dancing all over them.

"You know," said Angela, as we leaned over the railings to catch the breeze, "I'm not really into concrete jungles, but this really is something else."

We took a short stroll down the Avenue of the Stars, where fans of Hong Kong's cinema could see handprints of their favourite actors. We didn't recognise anyone apart from Bruce Lee, who had his own statue, but every other visitor seemed to know who they were. People were pointing with glee at certain placards, the names of which we couldn't even read.

"So, out of the places we've been to so far," I said, "which has been your favourite?"

"Here," Angela answered immediately. "I love it. What about you?"

To me, it was between Bangkok and Siem Reap; I told Angela this. "I reckon I could live in Hong Kong, though. And there are not many places I can say that about."

We walked along the avenue, enjoying the gorgeous skyline opposite us. Eventually, we caught a tube back to the hotel.

7

The next day, Angela I and decided to visit Stanley.

Stanley was a town at the southern end of Hong Kong Island. Because our hotel was on the same island, we decided to catch a taxi there. The taxi driver's first name was Kong. It said so on his identification badge. I pointed it out to Angela who looked and nodded.

"He's called Kong," I whispered.

"Yeah, I know...so?"

"So it's Kong from Hong Kong. Or Hong Kong Kong."

Angela shook her head and stared outside, bored with my infantile mind.

Stanley had once been a thriving fishing village. But that was before the British arrived in the 19th century, and turned it into their administrative centre. Nowadays, though, Stanley is a retreat from the hustle and bustle of downtown Hong Kong. It has a nice little beach, and a pleasant waterfront lined with little bars and restaurants.

"Let's see the temple," said Angela, referring to the Tin Hau Temple we'd read about in the taxi. It was supposedly the oldest building in Hong Kong. "I want us to soak up a bit of culture while we're here in Hong Kong. It's not all about shopping and cable cars."

When we neared what we thought was the temple, Angela stopped. "That can't be it. It doesn't look old enough." She was right. The temple in front of us looked like it had been built only a decade previously. And to be truthful, it didn't look that inspiring either. But we went inside anyway, finding out it was the Tin Hau Temple, after all. The interior was a small, square room filled with statues of gods, devils and ships: all very interesting, but not particularly exciting.

"Hello," said a teenage girl sitting in the corner of the temple. We hadn't even noticed her. She gestured towards a box that said: DONATION. We pretended we didn't know what she meant and studied a framed piece of tiger skin. The sign said that an Indian policeman had shot the tiger in front of the Stanley Police Station in 1942.

"Hello," said the girl again. She was carrying the box towards us. She tapped it, and stood waiting. Angela put ten Hong Kong dollars (85p) in, and then we left.

"Well, that wasn't worth the effort," said Angela. "Let's find somewhere else."

8

After lunch, we headed to a long line of ferry piers. Our destination was Cheung Chau Island. The crossing went pleasingly quickly, and, before we knew it, the boat was spilling us out into a crowded area of seafront shops and bars. In the backstreets, fortune-tellers and old folk were sitting in doorways; as we wandered past, some of them stared.

"It reminds me of Whitby," I said to Angela, referring to the small British seaside town. Like Whitby, Cheung Chau seemed to have retained some of its former past, with narrow alleyways full of small shops and a harbour full of fishing boats. Also like Whitby, the island had been the haunt of pirates and smugglers. They hid their loot inside the numerous caves dotting the island.

We found a bar and soaked up the atmosphere. Hong Kong was full of different flavours. One minute you could be gazing up at a glass skyscraper, and the next you could be watching a man walking past with a tray of fish balanced on his head. Somehow, Hong Kong had managed to get the balance right between modern commercial splendour and cultural heritage.

"I think we should go to Macau tomorrow," I said, taking a sip of some Chinese-made beer.

"Why? What's there?"

"Casinos. But it also has a nice old town. Plus, if we don't go now, we'll probably never get the chance again."

Angela nodded, watching as a teenage couple wandered past. The girl had spiky red hair and was wearing some sort of punk-themed school uniform. Her boyfriend was dressed equally wackily. He was sporting a cowboy hat and green trousers.

"And the ferry only takes an hour," I added.

"Okay. Sounds good to me."

9

On the other side of the Cheung Chau Island was a small but busy beach. People were packed together sunbathing, or swimming in the warm sea. One man, propelling himself along on a bright pink lilo, suddenly keeled into the water in a most comical fashion. It was like a shark had got him. He splashed to the surface and clambered back aboard.

We arrived at a section of Cheung Chau Island dedicated to the sale of seafood. Small fish, large fish, brightly-coloured fish and ugly fish were in tanks outside restaurants. An elderly Chinese couple stopped at one of the tanks and pointed. The man in charge nodded and produced a large net. With his rubber boots and plastic bag, he stepped into the large tank, and, after capturing the fish, he led the couple inside the restaurant. It was definitely a fresh fish establishment.

Nearby was a large building that turned out to be an indoor meat market. Women were sitting on tall chairs hacking up large pieces of fish, and, further along, a man with a cigarette dangling from his mouth was chopping up a piece of tuna steak. "Right," I said. "Time to head back."

In an act of pure unrestrained lavishness, I upgraded our ferry seats from ordinary class to deluxe class. Angela was excited. It wasn't often we were able to lord it past the people in the cheap seats, and, as we marched by them, I couldn't help but gloat. We climbed some steps and found ourselves on an open-air deck. Our deluxe seats offered a fantastic view of the island as we left the harbour. The sun was setting, fishing boats were sailing past, and, with the wind in our hair, it was just about perfect.

"How much did it cost to upgrade?" Angela asked.

I told her that the cost didn't matter; the only issue was that she was comfortable. "For you, my darling, no cost is too great."

"Come on," she pressed. "How much was it?"

I had no choice but to come clean. "Forty pence."

"Forty pence for all this! What a bargain!"

We sailed onwards to Hong Kong Island. The next day was our trip to Macau.

Bangkok

Clockwise from top left: The temples of the Grand Palace; Angela and I pose on top of Wat Arun; Young monks of Bangkok; Puppies for sale in Chatuchak Weekend Market; Heading into the Patpong district; Giant Reclining Buddha

Vientiane

Clockwise from top left: Patuxai Monument; Angela about to release some birds; Street scene from downtown Vientiane; A trio of Buddhist monks; Tuk-tuk driver asleep in the back of his vehicle; Beer Lao; Me standing in front of Pha That Luang

Hanoi

Clockwise from top left: The pastel-coloured buildings of Da Nang; Halong Bay; Street side fish peddlers in Hanoi; Motorbikes are everywhere in Vietnam; Angela enjoying the scenery from inside a taxi; Mausoleum of Ho Chi Minh

Siem Reap

Clockwise from top left: The classic Angkor Wat shot; Floating village near Siem Reap; Tacky touristy shot taken at the Angkor Wat complex; Dead Fish Restaurant; Two monks walk inside Angkor Wat; Crocodile farm; Local girls try to sell bangles to Angela (she bought lots)

Phnom Penh

Clockwise from top left: The Royal Palace; Angela enjoying an evening drink in Phnom Penh; The boys on the boat next to ours; Waitress from the Pyongyang North Korean Restaurant; One of the torture cells from Tuol Sleng Prison; Monks wandering along Sisowath Quay; Victims of the Khmer Rouge

Phuket

Clockwise from top left: The beauty of the Andaman Sea off Phuket; Our private beach; The jetty where we saw a sea snake; I pose in Phuket; This critter was as big as my hand; Sunburn from HELL!

Hong Kong

Clockwise from top left: A ferry speeds past the skyline of Hong Kong; Temple Street Night Market; Ngong Ping 360 cable car; Angela enjoying the view at the Peak; Hong Kong has beaches!; Cheung Chau; Neon lights of Kowloon

Chapter 8. Sweating in Macau

First established as a trading post in the sixteenth century, Macau (or Ultra Marino, as it was then called) had been a Portuguese colony until 1999. That was when they handed it back to China. Angela and I made our way to the ferry dock in Hong Kong, excited at the prospect of visiting another Special Administrative Region of China, this one only 40km away.

Our journey there promised to take only one hour, and, as we sped along, I began to watch the in-sail-entertainment. A Japanese television program had pitted man against bear. They were not fighting each other in the traditional sense, but were battling it out in a ferocious hotdog-eating contest.

At first, the young Japanese man seemed to be doing well, using the two-hotdogs-at-once method. They disappeared down his throat in quick and impressive succession. The bear, meanwhile, (bound by ropes on the other side of a partition) was leisurely chomping away on the occasional hotdog, not really bothered by all the fuss. A few minutes later, the man was still going strong and seemed a dead cert, even though he was now sweating. The score was 12:4 to the man.

As the contest heated up, the bear finally worked up more of an appetite. With the man slowing down, gulping breaths of air and rubbing his stomach, the bear scoffed a few hotdogs down, one after the other. The score was 18:7. The bear was speeding up.

Then, something seemed to change in the bear's demeanour. Instead of being almost sloth-like in its eating, it suddenly became focussed. Like a beast possessed, it turned into a hotdog-eating machine, devouring tubes of sausage like never before. With the seconds ticking down, the man slowed further, looking almost on the point of throwing up, but the bear kept up the pace. By the end, the bear had munched through fifty hotdogs compared to the man's paltry thirty-eight.

2

"Why do they bother having passport control?" asked Angela, which was a valid question since Macau and Hong Kong were essentially the same country. I told her I didn't know, as we joined the back of a long queue. Not only did Macau have its own border control, it had its own police, its own flag and its own airline.

The day we chose to visit Macau turned out to be a hot one. The temperature was intense as we left the ferry terminal, and, together with the high humidity, it turned us into sweating wrecks, especially me. As we walked past the lines of free buses waiting to transport people to casinos, I could feel the sweat dribbling down my back.

At first glance, Macau seemed to be cut from the same piece of cloth as Hong Kong, but, when we looked closer, there were two noticeable differences. Firstly, the buildings (with the exception of the casinos and posh hotels) were noticeably shabbier; some of them looked like they could do with a good clean. And secondly, the streets they stood upon were not as clean as Hong Kong's, often with litter and the occasional smattering of graffiti.

"Do you know where we're going?" asked Angela. "I need to get in some shade soon."

We were walking along a busy road flanked by casinos. A large one with *Sands* emblazoned across it was on our left-hand side. Reflective golden glass covered its exterior. I looked at the map again; Sands wasn't on it. To be honest, I didn't really know where we were. I gazed up at the sun, but wished I hadn't. Spots of white immediately flickered across my vision. We trudged onwards.

3

Ten minutes later, I spotted two people standing outside another large hotel and casino. The man and woman were wearing some sort of uniform: employees of the hotel, most probably porters. Just then, a bus pulled up. Under the direction of the uniformed porters, a contingent of Chinese men trooped off and entered the building.

"Hi," I said to the porters. "I wonder if you could help me?"

The woman glanced at me briefly but then turned her attention back onto the road. Her colleague didn't even bother looking.

"Hi," I said again. "Do you speak English?"

"No," said the woman, scouring the road for more coaches.

"Okay, but can you tell me where Senado Square is?"

The woman shook her head, and the man finally spoke. "We no speak English. You go!"

What a bloody cheek! Angela looked as incredulous as I did. I wondered whether to pull the man's silly hat off.

"Thanks," I said, as we walked away. "It was a pleasure speaking with you."

4

The heat was getting worse as we traipsed through downtown Macau. We considered jumping in a taxi, but felt we were so close to the centre that it probably wasn't worth it. Growing ever thirstier, we bought a bottle of water each from a street kiosk. I downed mine in seconds. My T-shirt was drenched, and sweat was seeping into my eyes. It made it hard to stare at the casinos.

Macau's economy is based on the gambling industry. It surprised me to know that, since 2006, Macau has taken more revenue from its casinos than Las Vegas. Some of Macau's casinos looked fairly classy; others looked tacky to the extreme. The biggest offender in the latter category was the Grand Lisboa Hotel and Casino, a gigantic golden thing that jutted out above the other skyscrapers. It looked like a cross between a supersized Christmas bauble and an enormous football trophy. I thought it looked fantastic, but Angela thought it an eyesore.

And then, by pure chance, we stumbled upon Senado Square. It was a picturesque part of the city, flanked by brightly painted colonial buildings. A fountain stood in its centre, which was surrounded by people with cameras. We moved on, coming to a section of town full of narrow streets and shops. We passed a stall selling slabs of deep-fried meat. They were very popular, even though they looked like shiny pieces of pink plastic.

Up a slight incline lay the ruins of Saint Paul's Cathedral. As the most iconic sight of Macau (apart from the casinos), plenty of people were crawling over its steps. We joined them.

"Look at your trousers!" exclaimed Angela. She was walking behind me. "They're soaked. It looks like you've wet yourself!"

I tried to look, but my neck was incapable of swivelling that far. Instead, Angela took a photo so I could see. She was right: a dark, wet patch of scrotal sweat. It felt sticky and horrible, and all I wanted to do was jump into the sea, or else have a shower.

"Why are you sweating so much?" my wife asked.

"I don't know. Probably because it's so hot and we've walked bloody miles."

Feeling self-conscious, I walked up the remaining steps with my hands clasped behind my back. It occurred to me that this might draw more attention, but I didn't care.

"Just walk normally," suggested Angela. "No one is looking."

Finally, we reached the cathedral ruins.

5

Imagine a church. Now imagine if every section of it crumbed to the ground, all except for the front part. That is what the ruins of Saint Paul's Cathedral look like. A fire had caused the destruction in 1835.

Fancy columns and numerous statues decorated the remaining section. But the best thing was the sunlight streaming through the open windows. Suddenly, I heard laughter and spun around, paranoid about my sweat patch. But it was a group of teenagers messing about on the steps.

"Come on," said Angela. "Let's find the lighthouse."

Guia Lighthouse, another of Macau's most visible landmarks, was on top of a large hill. To get there, we had to hike up a long winding pathway that increased the level of sweat saturation on my already-drenched clothes. There was supposed to be a cable car to the top, but we hadn't spotted any sign of one, which annoyed me. My head was throbbing, and my ears were pulsing, but the worst thing was my testicles. They were marinating in a salty brew furnaced by the frictional heat of movement. By the time we reached the summit, I looked a wreck. But at least I'd given up trying to hide the patches. If people spotted them, so be it.

6

The lighthouse sat at the highest point in Macau, and had been flashing its lights since 1638. It was rather small, but it looked well kept, covered in white paint. It had some nice arched windows, and I had to concede that it looked like a good lighthouse. It was so famous that it actually featured on the front of the ten pataca note.

Next to it was a church, and all around were some old Portuguese battlements, which included a wall and a cannon. The view spanned much of the city, and, as we stared out across the forest of skyscrapers, we noticed the gigantic golden ornament that masqueraded itself as the Grand Lisboa Casino again.

"Why would they build something like that?" Angela asked. "It's hideous."

"I love it. If we were stopping the night, that's where we'd be staying."

We headed around the other side of the complex, where we found the cable car station – so it did exist. After the short journey down the wires, we decided to make our way back to the ferry terminal. There didn't seem much more to do in Macau, and, besides, it was getting quite late.

7

As we sat in the air-conditioned deck of the jetfoil, my sweat patch began to recede. As it did so, it was leaving behind a cruel sting in the tail, because, as the moisture evaporated, tiny salt crystals were forming. They were clinging to my delicate upper thigh areas, waiting for the opportunity to bite.

Back at the ferry terminal in Hong Kong, I was about to experience new realms of pain. In fact, the resulting chafing was pure agony. It was like a set of razor blades cutting into my legs.

"Ahhh," I moaned with every faltering step, inhaling sharply whenever my upper legs made contact with each other. "Eeeeh!" I screeched with every movement. With a long hike to the tube station, I either had to walk wide-legged (like an exaggerated John Wayne) or else shuffle forward using tiny steps (like a broken robot). In the end, I did a mixture of these until we finally got back to the hotel.

Worse was to come the next day. I rose from the bed and almost fell to the ground again. The pain was mesmerizingly bad. I couldn't even walk to the shower without Angela helping me. And the hot water didn't help. I screamed like a lunatic.

"I need socks," I shouted to Angela from the bathroom afterwards. "Two tied together, end on end."

"What?"

"Pass me some socks, will you? Two pairs please."

Since we didn't possess any bandages, and a quick trip to the local supermarket was out of the question, I had been forced to improvise. Like a member of the A-Team, I fashioned a sock bandage, which I wrapped around my upper thighs, and then tied together in a loose knot. Disturbingly, when I caught sight of myself in the mirror, it looked like I was wearing suspenders. God help me if I was involved in some sort of traffic accident and had to be taken to hospital. Tentatively, I got dressed.

"And now for the moment of truth," I said to Angela, as I took a small step forward, ready to halt the instant any pain was felt. But I felt nothing. I was a new man!

Angela smiled. "So this means we can go out now?"

"Of course," I said, bounding around the room. "We can go jogging if you want."

Outside, on the busy streets of downtown Hong Kong, I confidently strode about like a man with no chafing whatsoever, even taking lolloping strides to show off my newfound freedom of movement.

"No!" I said five minutes later. I'd just felt the bandage on my right leg come undone, and could feel it slipping down my thigh. I caught it just in time (by placing my hand over my pocket area), but was then presented by a further dilemma. Should I let the socks slide down my trouser leg, and then pull them out like a demented snake charmer, or was it better to hold them in position? In the crowds of Hong Kong, I had to act quickly, and so elected to hold the bandage in position. But the pain was the worst thing. The chafing was back with vengeance. We headed back to the hotel and I whimpered pathetically all the way.

"Well, next stop Tokyo," I said when I'd bandaged myself up properly. There was no way my suspenders were going to slip down now.

Angela clapped her hands. "I know! I'm so excited. Japan is somewhere I've wanted to go since I was a little girl. I can't wait."

We packed our bags in preparation for our afternoon flight. Little did I know that my chafing was about to set new standards in agony.

Chapter 9. The land of the Robotic Toilets

The first confirmed notion about how courteous and well-mannered Japanese people were was at the check-in desk for our Japan Airlines flight to Tokyo. As we waited for the desks to open, a line of Japanese check-in agents trooped down some steps; all impeccably dressed and armed with beaming smiles. After lining up in front of us, they bowed and thanked us for choosing their airline.

Going through airport security at Hong Kong International, I had an incident. It involved my chafing bandages. An overzealous security official frisked me and felt the bumpy bit through one of my trouser legs. It was the section of bandage I'd tied into a tight knot. He felt it again, and then looked at me. "What is that?" he asked, prodding the knot.

My mouth went dry. "A bandage."

The man looked sceptical. "A bandage? A bandage for what? And why is it like that?"

I looked around for Angela. She was in the queue next to me, taking off her shoes. She had no idea of my anguish. I suddenly had a vision of me standing there with my trousers around my ankles, my homemade suspender belt on show for all to see. People would be gawping and pointing at the English pervert in their midst, shielding their children's eyes from the ghastly sight. And then Angela would see.

I looked at the security guard, embarrassment seeping from every pore. "For my sore thighs," I said. "My wife and I did a lot of walking yesterday. In Macau. It was really hot."

The man felt the knot again, and then ran his hand around the length of the bandage. He did the same on the other leg. "Go," he finally said, shaking his head. "Just go."

I collected my belongings, and rushed away. I then paused for Angela to arrive, and when she did, I hung my head in shame.

2

Just the name, Tokyo, sounded high tech. The Japanese capital was the land of the gadget and gizmo. Narita Airport lived up to this image: full of flashing signs and whirring escalators. After being stamped into the country by an extremely polite customs official, Angela and I wandered towards the baggage carousels.

"Excuse me," said a quiet voice.

We turned to see an airport policeman standing behind us. He bowed.

"I am sorry to take up your time," he said, "but I need to ask you a few security questions. Is this okay with you?"

We both nodded, and so he asked us where we had come from and where we were staying. He wrote our answers down on a little form. Afterwards he bowed again and thanked us. We couldn't help but be impressed.

3

We were soon on the Narita Express, the fastest way into the city. And then, one hour later, after negotiating our way out of Tokyo Central Station, we jumped in a taxi to the Asakusa district of Tokyo, a twenty-minute drive from the centre. Our driver looked like a Bond villain. His squat face and blocky shoulders made him a double for Oddjob, henchman to Goldfinger. He was wearing a white shirt, a black tie, gloves and a fixed expression. His taxi was like all the others in downtown Tokyo – a box-like Toyota Comfort. Inside looked better though, full of electronic gadgetry. Buttons here, flashing lights there. I was surprised it didn't have an ejector seat.

The streets of downtown Tokyo were busy, but well ordered. Long gone was the incessant beeping of Thailand and Vietnam; instead, the roads were full of modern eco-friendly cars keeping excellent lane discipline. As well as the vehicles, there were plenty of people too. Like ants, they marched along, or sometimes crowded at intersection, all under the glare offered by gigantic TV screens and flashing neon advertisements. Eventually we arrived outside the Chisun Inn. It had the smallest rooms in the world.

4

"Have you seen the size of this?" asked Angela in a pained voice after we'd dragged our suitcases inside the room. The bed took up most of the space, and there was hardly any room for the luggage. "And this wardrobe's a joke!"

I looked at the offending article, but couldn't see it. All I could see was a box about thirty centimetres wide, reaching from the floor to the ceiling.

"Well there's no room for any of your clothes in here," warned Angela. "I'll tell you that now."

Despite the minuscule size of the room, it did have one incredible plus, and it was located in the bathroom. I wasted no time at all in trying it out. It thrilled me when a jet of water tickled my nether regions, and so I pressed another button to see what would happen next. A sprinkling, and then a whooshing torrent erupted. I giggled with childish delight. I'd seen toilets such as this on TV but couldn't believe we had one in our room! I pressed another button and turned a dial. The effect was amazing. Even getting my sock suspenders a little wet did not dampen my amusement.

"I think I'm going to like Tokyo," I said a few minutes later, squeezing past Angela who was squashing some clothes into the tiny wardrobe.

"What were you doing in there? It sounded like you were flushing the toilet over and over."

"I was playing with the robotic toilet. It's the best invention ever."

I walked to our small window and opened the curtains. The view wasn't great because it overlooked the side of the adjacent building. But a pair of pink slippers dangling from the window opposite caught my eyes. They were close enough to touch. Wondering why someone had put them there, I closed the curtains and went back to the bathroom. I had to have another go.

5

The next morning we were off, negotiating the confusing subway system back to central Tokyo. The map we were using had the whole scheme on one page and looking at it made my eyes water. It resembled a pile of coloured spaghetti splashed all over the place. In our confusion, we resorted to asking random strangers for help, and each one was helpful and well-mannered, pointing this way or that, and then bowing afterwards. The Japanese were really the nicest people on Earth.

Tokyo Central Station was a hive of super activity, and as we stood in the middle getting our bearings, we were surrounded by streams of people rushing past in every direction. Along the edge of the concourse, shops and cafes were in abundance, and everything was spotlessly clean. We spied an exit sign and headed towards it. My chafing bandages were still working a treat, and most of the soreness had now gone. Before leaving the hotel, I'd applied healthy dollops of anti-chafing cream too. Soon I'd be able to abandon the bandages altogether.

Above ground, a hot and humid August morning in Tokyo awaited us. We took to the streets, heading towards Ginzo, the shopping district of the city. "Do you think the women here are attractive?" Angela asked, as a bevy of beauties came from the opposite direction.

I didn't know whether it was a trick question, and so was unsure how to answer. Japanese women *were* attractive. I'd noticed that already. But should I admit that to my wife?

"Because I do," said Angela. "Their skin is so good, and they have such striking features."

"Oh? I hadn't noticed."

Ginzo was made up of large department stores, all offering designer goods and basement eateries. Each of the restaurants featured plastic mock-ups of the food for sale. Someone was making a lot of money from these plastic meals, I mused. They were in every eatery in the city, despite making some of the food look extremely unappetising. One pretend plate was full of plastic noodles, with a shiny fried egg on top. Ribbons of synthetic tomato ketchup covered it all. Another artificial meal was laid out in different sections. One featured a slice of plastic lemon with strings of shiny lettuce. The battered chicken leg was less convincing, though. We decided to leave the plastic food restaurants alone for the time being.

After wandering around a few stores, we entered the Sony Building, a six-storey department store filled with gadgets. My personal favourites were the 3D computer games. But I was also taken with a large tank of water. Inside, were lifelike, remote-controlled fish. Teenagers with consoles were making them attack each other. It was amazing to think how far computing had come since I'd played games in the 1980s.

6

Tokyo, it came as no surprise, was expensive. Our yen was disappearing with lightning speed, and soon we needed more. The ATM we found wouldn't accept either of our cards and so we tried another. It spat them out with the same result. At the third machine, we got the satisfying rumbling of cash about to be dispensed, but were ultimately thwarted by the screen saying: CARD NOT ACCEPTED.

"Why have they got calculators on them?" asked Angela as we approached the fourth ATM. I'd noticed the calculators too. They were embedded into every machine we'd seen.

"No idea." I couldn't think of any possible function, apart from as a currency converter. Just then, the ATM rumbled and sprung into life. Precious banknotes appeared from within. The only problem was they were 10000 Yen notes, worth over $100 each.

"Well, at least we've got some cash now," I said, stuffing the notes into my wallet. Twenty minutes later, we were travelling by metro back to Asakusa.

7

The evening streets of Asakusa were busy. After dropping off a few things in our room, we were wandering past karaoke bars, cupcake shops and a strange shop that had a collection of life-sized plastic superheroes outside. I posed near Ultraman, a 1960s Japanese superhero whose special powers included the *Ultra Punch* (with the power of 50 Indian elephants), and the *Ultra Chop* (a monster-defeating karate chop that also created a flash of energy upon impact). But perhaps his greatest strength was the power of *Ultra Separation*. When confronted with more than one monster, Ultraman could create four duplicates of himself. I put my hand on his silver shoulder and smiled while Angela took a photo.

Historically, Asakusa had been one of the main pleasure districts of Tokyo (i.e. entertainment districts), but after massive aerial bombing during the Second World War had flattened most of it, Asakusa has become more sedate.

The most famous sight is the Senso-Ji Buddhist Temple, Japan's oldest. Stalls filled the avenue leading to it, selling chopsticks, paper lanterns and, curiously, items of clothing for dogs. People huddled around the aisles, most of them locals.

"It looks amazing," said Angela as we regarded the large red and white shrine in front of us. It had one of those tapering

Oriental roofs that always look exotic to Western eyes. And arriving after sunset had been a great idea, because it was so beautifully lit. Just along from it was a towering golden pagoda. Its five-layered roof shone like a beacon.

Behind the temple was a busy street full of cafes and bars, as well as strip clubs and porn theatres. Nude young women covered a large advertising board outside one such establishment. There were also slot machine emporiums everywhere. Whenever their automatic doors opened to let someone in or out, we caught glimpses of people huddled at sparkly machines, bathed in artificial light. The noise they were being subjected to was the worst kind of electronic music possible. As soon as the doors swept shut, the hellish vision and cacophony was gone.

We also noticed quite a few women wearing the traditional Japanese kimono. They looked almost doll-like, especially with their painted white faces. Many of them carried dainty umbrellas. Whether the women were there for the tourists or for real, we had no idea. After a bite to eat (where we pointed at some plastic food to make our order), we retired back to the Chisun Inn.

8

The next morning, we caught a river cruise along the Sumida River. Apart from apartment blocks and skyscrapers, there wasn't much to see. Compounding matters was the lady at the front with the microphone. She only spoke Japanese, and so, even if we were passing interesting monuments, we couldn't tell. Thirty minutes later, we alighted and found ourselves in a park full of chirping insects and beautiful butterflies.

The park was actually called the Hama Rikyu Garden. It was where Imperial Guards had once come to shoot ducks. Appropriately enough, we didn't see any ducks there at all. We followed everybody else through the park until we arrived at a huge meadow of orange and yellow flowers. It buzzed with the sound of insects.

"We need to catch a tube," I said, after finally working out our location.

Angela bent down to take a photo of a large purple butterfly. It fluttered off in the haphazard way all butterflies do before she could focus on it. "Where are we going next?" she asked, straightening up.

"The Imperial Palace Gardens."

"Sounds good. I've always wondered what the Emperor's palace looks like."

I shook my head. "We won't be able to see it. It's off limits to the public. But the gardens are supposed to be nice."

Forty minutes later, we were a bit bored. Apart from stone battlements and deep moats, there was not much to do inside the Imperial Gardens. In fact, the most interesting thing had been a group of teenagers we passed near the entrance. They had been practising some sort of martial art with long sticks.

"Shall we go to Shibuya?" I suggested.

"Yeah. Good idea."

9

We emerged from the underground into the maddest pedestrian crossing in the world. The Shibuya Crossing was insane. Hundreds of people were crisscrossing each other under the glow of some giant video screens. Angela and I stared at the scene, smiling to ourselves. Whenever travel programs broadcast footage of Tokyo, they always show the Shibuya Crossing, usually speeded up. It looked amazing.

Around the edge of the huge square were high-rise department stores, catering mainly for the young and trendy of Tokyo. A geisha woman in traditional costume walked past. She had a delicate fan and some flowers in her hair. She joined the throng of people crossing the road, soon disappearing among teenage girls wearing white shirts, short black pleated skirts and hair tied in bunches. Most of the girls were also sporting black ties and knee-length black socks. As it was a Saturday, they were not in school uniform.

While Angela went to look around some shops, I was deposited in a cafe filled with teenagers eating cheesecake. I bagged a window seat so I could watch the crossing from above. From my new perspective, it looked even more frenzied.

I opened the guidebook, looking for places to visit next. I thought the famous Tsukiji Fish Market might be worth a trip, and seeing sumo wrestlers might be fun too. I also looked for places where we could get a good view of the city from, and settled for a building called the Mori Tower. It had an observation deck at the top.

Half an hour later, Angela returned with a few gifts for people back home, mainly chopsticks. After I told her of the three places we could visit, she scrunched up her face. "Sumo wrestling?" Why would I want to see that?"

"Because it'll be funny."

Angela looked at me incredulously. "How so?"

"I don't know...? Two fat men fighting...?"

"Well you can go by yourself, then."

She did agree with the other two suggestions, though. But when we looked for more information on the fish market, we discovered it was only open in the morning. We decided we would see it the next day. So that left the Mori Tower, a 54-storey silver skyscraper. We headed for the underground once more.

Astonishingly, there was no queue to get up to the sky deck. We walked into the empty lift and were soon ascending at a dizzying pace. At the top, we went straight to the window, staring out over the city. Tokyo sprawled for miles in every direction.

After wandering around the unimpressive Mori Tower Art Gallery, we returned to the observation deck. The sun was going down, and as it did so, the lights of Tokyo came on. They looked spectacular. We watched as twinkling aircraft made their approach into Haneda Airport, and then, when it was completely dark, we made our way to the elevator. It was time to go back to the hotel.

10

"Will you stop using that bloody toilet!" said Angela when I emerged from it the next morning. I was addicted to the thing, and had been in and out four times already. "It's disturbing me."

"It's only disturbing because you can't work out how to use it."

After breakfast in a nearby Starbucks, we were back in the underground on our way to the fish market. In 2010, the Tokyo authorities had temporarily banned tourists from the Tsukiji Fish Market. They were sick of people interfering with the early morning tuna auctions. Though the ban had been lifted, Angela and I got the distinct impression from the people working there (most of them cigarette-smoking, hard-looking men), that our presence was not welcome. Unlike every other Japanese person we'd come across, the men in the fish market were unfriendly, glaring and shaking their heads as we passed.

The best time to visit the fish market was early in the morning. Auctions started at just past 5am, and ended by 7am. The best Angela and I could manage was 10am. We had missed the crowds and now stood out like sore thumbs.

Beep, came the sound from our rear. We moved to the side as a mechanical cart carrying boxes of fish sped through the aisle. The driver looked at us angrily as he manoeuvred past.

"Who can blame them for not wanting us here?" said Angela, as we walked past a couple of large fish heads. "They're trying to do their jobs, and we're blocking the aisles and taking photos."

I nodded, wandering over to some large white polystyrene boxes filled with squid, crabs and some strange round black things covered with spikes. They looked like some sort of sea anemone. Whatever the creatures were, they cost 250 yen (£1.70) each.

"So you're definitely not interested in some sumo wrestling?" I asked, as we passed a stall with an upturned tuna head on display. It looked gruesome. I was about to take a photo but a man in a white apron glared.

"No. It sounds boring."

"Well, I can't go by myself."

"Why not?"

I stopped walking and turned to my wife.

"Because people will think I'm strange. A bloke turning up by himself to watch some near-naked men having a fight; that's not normal is it?"

"Neither is using a toilet ten times a day just so you can try all the buttons. And that's not stopped you."

As it turned out, there wasn't any sumo wrestling going on, anyway. For a start, the sumo tournaments only occurred three times a year (January, May and October) and, though the wrestlers sometimes trained at other times of the year, they usually finished by nine in the morning. Sumo and tuna, it appeared, were early morning activities in Tokyo.

11

For lunch, Angela and I decided to go for a meal close to our hotel. Once again, we had to rely on pointing at the plastic plates, hoping that the real things would be more appetising than the models.

Angela was quite happy with her choice, some deep fried pieces of pork and rice, but I was disappointed with mine, especially the random slices of tentacle, and indescribable purple bits of rubber that were in my boiled egg soup. I hadn't seen those in the plastic mock-up. Nevertheless, I picked up my chopsticks and started eating.

Before visiting Japan, I could count on my fingers the number of times I'd used chopsticks, but now I was a dab hand. Like the locals, my face was bent low, almost at the rim of my cruel gruel, and with a constant hand motion of chopstick to mouth, I could get the noodles and suckers into my chops with only the minimum of mess.

"I've really enjoyed Tokyo," I said to Angela on the way back to the Chisun Inn. "I like the people, and I like the fact it's so organised. This has been my favourite place so far."

"I think Hong Kong was better."

I shook my head. "No, Hong Kong was just a huge Asian city. It was great, don't get me wrong, but it didn't have the distinct culture of Tokyo. I mean, if we showed someone a photo of Hong Kong, and asked people where they thought it was, some might guess Shanghai or maybe Singapore. But Tokyo looks like Tokyo, and I like that."

We arrived back into our tiny room and began packing again. Later that evening, we were heading to the airport for the next stage of our adventure: Taiwan. After a final go on the best toilet in the world, I helped Angela pack the suitcases.

Chapter 10. Fried Fish Lips in Taipei

"This is beyond a joke," I said, sweat dripping down my face, my T-shirt already sodden.

Since getting off the airport bus at Taipei Central Station, Angela and I had dragged our sorry suitcases through the neon-lit centre of downtown Taipei, wondering how we would ever find the hotel. After lugging the un-luggable luggage up and down an underpass, I was ready to give up.

"This map is useless!" I exclaimed. Droplets of moisture sprayed from my nose as I whipped my head from side to side. I was like a man possessed. "We're totally lost, and totally hot, and we should've just got in a bloody taxi!"

"It was your idea to get the bus," snapped Angela. She was as hot and bothered as I was. "So don't get angry with me."

"I'm not angry with you."

"You sound like it."

I stared around, trying to spot a street sign in the darkened streets of Taipei. There was none that I could see. I glared at the map again, a hateful piece of clammy paper that was about as useful as cholera. On it, the hotel looked tantalisingly close to the central station – just along that street and down that road. But what it didn't factor in were the tropical temperature, some hellish humidity, and a total lack of situational awareness.

"Damn Taiwan!" I snarled. "And damn this map."

2

The only thing I knew about Taiwan, apart from the fact that it was also called the Republic of China, was that a lot of electronic toys from my childhood had been made there. In the late Seventies, Taiwan became synonymous with cheap but quality high-tech goods, and it seemed nothing much had changed. The shops we were passing were full of electronic gadgetry. Taiwan's electrical exports had made it one of the richest countries in Asia.

Except it isn't really a country. Not exactly, anyway. China does not recognise Taiwan's independence and nor does the USA or UK. In fact, only 23 countries do recognise Taiwan, mostly in Central America and the Pacific Ocean. That said, most countries do have some sort of unofficial relationship with Taiwan, allowing trade and commerce to occur. Even China has relaxed its feelings towards what it has historically considered a breakaway state. It now allows direct flights between Beijing and Taipei, something that had been banned for half a century. Taiwan has its own currency, government, economy, police force and borders. In almost every way, it *is* a country. Except it isn't. Sort of.

3

"Jesus Christ!" I said as we dragged our suitcases past an endless array of camera shops. Did they really need so many camera shops in one concentrated area? "Where the hell is the bloody hotel?"

We stopped to take our bearings again. The map might as well have been blank for all the help it was offering. Platoons of scooters zipped past, racing off along the street. I looked for a taxi, but none seemed to be passing down the street we were on.

"Just calm down," said Angela, "and stop shouting."

I glared at my wife, trying to turn my ire down a notch. "I'm not shouting," I said through clenched teeth.

Angela looked at the map. Just then, a man approached. He climbed off his bicycle and asked if we needed help. We nodded gratefully and I told him the name of the hotel. The man shook his head. He had never heard of it. When I told him the address, he rubbed his head and thought for a moment. "I think, that way," he said, pointing along a side street. We thanked him and trudged off. Within minutes, we were lost again.

A young woman came to our assistance next, quickly joined by a middle-aged man, and then a passing motorcyclist. The last arrival proved most useful. He'd actually heard of the hotel, and after checking something on his phone, he rang them, asking for accurate directions.

"Very near," he said putting his phone back in his pocket. "Down there and then turn right." He pointed to a tiny street we'd been about to walk past.

We thanked our rescue party and wandered off, and then, like a mirage, we found Paradise. The two-star Paradise Hotel had been hidden behind some taller buildings all the time.

4

The next morning was rainy and humid, with the odd rumble of thunder thrown in for good measure. The Paradise Hotel was a basic affair, smelling of dampness along its corridors, but it was located in the middle of a bustling street, complete with food vendors and electronic shops. Just along from it was a teeming shopping arcade full of young people out to bag a bargain. "It reminds me of Hong Kong, or maybe Bangkok," I said as we passed chop shops peddling their food to passing pedestrians.

"Yeah," agreed Angela. "With a bit of Hanoi mixed in for good measure."

Scooters whizzed past us as we tried to cross the road, and unlike the previous evening, yellow taxis were everywhere. The cars seemed modern, and the roads and pavements of good quality. Starbucks, McDonalds and KFCs were also in abundance. People were all around us, but hardly any were foreigners.

Despite the obvious wealth in the city (the glittering skyscrapers, the busy shopping malls, and the large outdoor video screens), some parts of Taipei looked in need of a paint job. Whereas Tokyo had been clean, cultured and classy, Taipei was rough and ready, not afraid to show its grime. Angela and I caught the cheap and efficient subway to our first tourist site of the day – the Kong Miao Confucius Temple.

5

Built in 1925, the Confucius Temple was located in a beautiful complex with other smaller temples and shrines. It even had a man playing a Chinese-style flute adding to the atmosphere. The roof of the temple was particularly impressive, curving upwards in that particular Chinese style that looked so distinctive. Serpents and dragons adorned sections of the roof, and the two large columns at the entrance had terrible creatures spiralling up along their lengths.

The complex had a Confucius Gift Shop and a little park adjoining it. The gift shop was full of Confucius-themed souvenirs, including porcelain cups, fridge magnets and school bags. There was even a Confucius USB flash drive, capable of holding an 'impressive amount of knowledge'. The nearby pool had a large dragon sending plumes of water from its nostrils. The water cascaded over the large goldfish that lived in the pond. Suddenly the loud roar of a jet engine cut through the tranquility, and we looked up to see an airliner making its approach into nearby Songshan Airport.

Next door was the two-hundred year old Baoan Temple, dedicated to the God of Medicine. This shrine was perhaps even more impressive than the Confucius Temple, filled with paper lanterns and people praying. A large table in front of the shrine was festooned with fruit, flowers and money: all offerings. The scent of incense hung in the air. Angela and I were the only tourists in attendance.

According to British Foreign Office Statistics, around 38,000 UK nationals visit Taiwan every year, and a lot of them are from the business world. Thailand gets over 800,000 British visitors and Hong Kong gets half a million. Even Japan, notoriously expensive and too far-flung for many people, gets almost four times as many visitors as Taiwan. Out of all the places we would visit on our trip around Asia, Taiwan was definitely the least visited.

As we wandered around the temple, the heat was really starting to get to me; my T-shirt was already soaked. Worried about the possibility of chafing again (I'd abandoned the bandages in Tokyo, and was now only using a strange gel that reduced all friction), we decided to leave. Above us, thunderclouds were forming, and so, to escape the upcoming tropical onslaught, we caught a taxi to the Grand Hotel, possibly the most famous hotel in Taipei.

6

When we arrived, both of us regarded the massive hotel standing before us. It did look quite impressive with its red and orange exterior, as well as its Chinese-style roof, apparently the world's biggest. In fact, it looked like a gigantic Chinese temple. Notable guests of the hotel included Richard Nixon, Bill Clinton, Margaret Thatcher and Nelson Mandela. We entered its air-conditioned interior and sat down; we were dismayed to find that, unlike the rest of Taipei, the prices inside the Grand Hotel were not cheap.

While we sipped our $250 (five pounds) glasses of orange juice, we looked in the guidebook for other places to visit.

"How about this?" I said to Angela, pointing at a photo. It showed a troop of splendid-looking soldiers about to change the guard. "It's called Martyrs Shrine and it's not far from here. But we'll have to be quick – they change the guard on the hour."

Angela looked at her watch and saw that it was ten to eleven. We paid our bill, rushed outside and hailed one of the waiting taxis.

"Martyrs Shrine," I said to the driver, showing him the photo in the book.

"Okay," he said nodding.

As we set off, I looked at my watch again. There were only six minutes left. I pulled a pained expression toward Angela, which the driver caught. He glanced at his dashboard clock and understood our plight.

"Do not worry," he said, pressing down hard on the accelerator. "Enough time."

He drove through the ever-darkening streets of Taipei like a maniac. He got us to the shrine with two minutes to spare. For that, he received a hearty tip.

7

"Was that it?" lamented Angela as we traipsed back towards the archway leading out of the Martyrs Shrine. I nodded glumly, putting my hat on to keep off the rain.

The changing of the guards was nothing like the book had suggested it would be. It had consisted of two teenage soldiers in white uniform stepping off some blocks, and then marching to a nearby guardhouse. It was all a big letdown really.

Still, the shrine itself had been interesting. It was a huge building with a sloping orange roof, containing the spirit tablets (placards dedicated to an ancestor) of almost 400,000 people killed in various wars and battles. Two fearsome stone lions guarded its entrance, and the hills surrounding the complex had looked lush and green, full to capacity with dense jungle.

With a terrific crash of thunder, the clouds suddenly decided to let rip. Instead of a light spattering of raindrops, they came down in a vertical sheet. We ran for the same taxi we'd arrived in; the driver had been waiting for us.

"Taipei 101," I said, already soaked to the skin

"Okay," he said. "This time I go slow!" He laughed at his own witticism.

Taipei 101 (named because of its 101 floors) was full of financial companies and designer goods malls; it also had an observation deck at the top. Two things put us off going up. Firstly, the overcast weather would not be great for panoramic views of the city, and secondly, there was a long queue waiting to board the elevators.

Instead, we found a cafe and ordered a coffee and a sandwich. Twenty minutes later, the rain had stopped sufficiently for us to venture back outside. We stared up at the fourth-highest building in the world.

"I don't know whether it looks good or not," I said. "It looks vaguely Chinese in design but very block-ish, as if it's been made from upside down noodle cartons." But it was hard not to be impressed with the size of Taipei 101, and the city as a whole, especially bearing in mind that, until as late as the 1960s, the city didn't even have a full set of paved roads.

8

That evening, we caught a tube to the Shilin Night Market, supposedly one of Taipei's top attractions. Before hitting the stalls, though, we decided to get something to eat. Bypassing street vendors selling noodles and tentacles, we opted for a traditional Taiwanese restaurant not far from the tube stop.

Boiled Cow's Hoof was one of the things on the menu, as was Stir-fried Pig Kidney with Chicken Testicles. If the title of the meal alone didn't whet the appetite, then the accompanying photo was sure to do it. I peered at the image, surprised to know that a chicken's testicle looked like a large piece of garlic. As I was pondering this delight, I turned the page and saw the piece de résistance of the menu: the mouth-watering Fish Lips in Casserole.

"My God," I said. "Have you seen this?" Angela giggled when she read it. I peered at the photo trying to make out the ingredients, but it just looked like a bowl of soup. I said, "Who in their right mind would eat fish lips? It reminds me of that place in Phnom Penh."

Despite the menu, or perhaps because of it, the place was packed with locals, all rubbing their chopsticks together with glee, in great anticipation of the feast ahead. We were the only foreigners in the place, and became the focus of attention from the waitresses.

I looked at one waitress to gesture we were ready to order, and she rushed over, notepad poised at the ready. When we told her our choice, another waitress hurried over to see what we'd picked. She looked disappointed when she saw we'd both ordered beef curry, the only normal thing on the menu.

Ten minutes later, our food arrived. It was horrible. Just a slimy mess of gruesome meat piled on top of some stodgy fried rice.

"I wish I'd gone for the fish lips, now," I said, using my chopsticks to examine a piece of fatty meat.

Suddenly there was a flash of light outside, closely followed by an almighty boom. Rain began to batter the windowpanes.

I picked up my bottle of beer and took a slurp. "I knew it," I said. "We're in Frankenstein's restaurant."

9

With our meal over, we had no choice but to head back outside. Because neither of us had brought coats, hats or umbrellas, we knew we were in for a soaking. More or less as soon as we stepped out, a sheet of tropical rain descended, coating us in fat blobs that splattered and drenched our clothes as we ran towards the night market.

A few minutes later, we were huddled under the awnings of a market stall. Everyone else was doing the same thing, watching as torrents of water flowed over pavements and roads. As we took stock of the situation, one of the flimsy plastic coverings above a nearby stall collapsed under the weight of the collecting water. The resulting waterfall drenched the woman just in front of us. She screamed and then stood there, eyes tightly shut, hands outstretched, as if she was having an electric shock.

Shilin Night Market was not that great. Instead of the bargains we'd been hoping for, it seemed to be an endless array of shoot-the-balloon-type stalls and noodle eateries. Cheesy pop music blared from tinny speakers, and after being jostled for the hundredth time, we decided to call it a day.

10

The next morning, following a suggestion from Angela, we caught a tube to the most northerly point on the city's subway system – a town called Tamsui. It was more like a suburb of Taipei than an actually defined town, but it did have a coastline on the East China Sea, as well as some scenic mountains in the background. That was why we'd decided to go.

Forty minutes later, we arrived. Tamsui was a popular destination; families were everywhere, and tour boats were plying the harbour front in full force. We walked along the crowded main street, and then decided to catch a small ferry to a place called Fisherman's Wharf. As we sat down for the short boat journey, an elderly Taiwanese gentleman approached us. For some reason he wanted to take our photograph.

While the other passengers looked on, Angela and I posed, and afterwards, he showed us the image. We nodded good-naturedly, and so the man showed us all the other photos on his camera. It was mostly of family members (we presumed), with the occasional photo of the man himself. As the boat set off, the old man tried telling us about the photos, but we couldn't understand a word of what he was saying. Eventually he gave up and sat across the aisle from us.

Soon after, we arrived at a wharf with a white bridge as its centrepiece. Everyone started to get off, and as the old man shuffled towards the exit, he looked back and smiled. We waved as he climbed out. When the boat was empty, we got off too, wondering where everyone had gone. Every passenger seemed to have disappeared into thin air. Only the driver remained. He was smoking a cigarette.

"Is this Fisherman's Wharf?" I asked him.

The man nodded and gestured all around.

"Where is everyone?"

The driver shrugged. "Gone."

Where, we wondered? No matter. Angela and I had a walk along the boardwalk, eventually stopping for a coffee in one of the overpriced cafes along it.

"It's a bit dead," Angela remarked.

I nodded, staring outside at the white bridge. The crossing looked sleek and modern. It seemed to be the only thing worth looking at in Fisherman's Wharf. Only later would we learn that Tamsui had an old Dutch fort, an old Presbyterian church and a few temples, but by then it was too late because we were on our way back to Taipei.

11

The next day, we made our way back to the airport. Instead of getting the bus, we stumped up the remaining Taiwanese dollars we had and booked a taxi.

On the way, we mused on our trip to Taiwan. Both of us agreed that, as a tourist destination, it was a bit lacking – there wasn't that much to see – at least as far as Taipei was concerned. Also, there was sometimes a certain *ripeness* to parts of the city, which may have been explained by the hot weather. But the worst thing for us was the food, or the lack of food catering to our western palates. Everywhere we'd eaten (apart from McDonald's one time) had been either a street vendor or a restaurant with a love of intestine. Angela summed up the visit to Taipei. "I've enjoyed being here for a few days, but I wouldn't ever come back."

Next stop was Manila, the capital of the Philippines.

Chapter 11. Onwards to Manila

Manila, the capital of the Philippines, will never top the list for places to visit. To many, the most densely populated city on Earth is a hotbed of street crime and violence, with appalling pollution and congested traffic. As well as that, it is supposedly full of slums and beggars. And besides, what is there to see? Virtually the whole city was bombed to obliteration during World War II, wasn't it?

Angela and I pondered this as we were sitting on our flight from Taiwan. But the real reason we were heading to the Philippines was to see a friend of ours called Andrew. He and I had taught at the same school in the UK, and had developed a keen friendship. When he'd decided that teaching was not for him, he'd reverted to his pre-education career in computing. Not long afterwards, he told me he was moving to Manila.

"Wow," I said, after he'd explained that he'd be working for an ICT training company over there.

"I know. The furthest I've been before is France. And that was by ferry."

"We'll have to come out and visit you."

Andrew smiled. "Lots of people have said that, but I think you're the only one who might actually do it."

Andrew was unmarried with no ties to the UK, and so the move was fairly painless for him. I was interested in catching up with him again. It was over a year since I'd seen him. I wanted to know what he thought of living in Manila.

2

During our approach into Ninoy Aquino International Airport, the number of skyscrapers in downtown Manila surprised me. From two thousand feet, the city looked like New York, albeit mixed in with some tropical greenery. Maybe the Philippines wasn't so poor, after all. After clearing customs, we were in Joe's taxi to the centre.

Taking in our surroundings up close, we noticed a few unsavoury elements to Manila creeping in. Shanty dwellings, together with people who looked homeless, seemed quite common beyond the airport. The air seemed thick with smog, coming mainly from the jeepneys.

"How long you in Manila?" asked Joe, pulling up at a thick line of traffic. The smoke pouring from one jeepney's exhaust was deplorable. A thick black tendril floated upwards into the hazy skies of downtown Manila.

"Two days," Angela answered.

"Two day? That's all? Not enough time!"

A three-wheeled vehicle drew alongside. It was piled with wooden crates filled with chickens. They were piled so high and wide that the vehicle looked like a gigantic box on wheels. The driver was standing up on his seat to see where he was going. As well as his cargo of chickens, he had two passengers along for the ride too.

"Nincompoop," said Joe, referring to the chicken driver. "But the police will not stop him. They never do."

Twenty minutes later, we arrived at the Hotel Miramar. The surrounding area looked decent enough. Tall, modern buildings and a wide highway were just along from the hotel, as was a lengthy ocean promenade. A line of palm trees added a touch of tropical beauty. The only worrying aspect was the armed guard standing at the Miramar's entrance. Next door, Starbucks had one too. Angela and I looked at each other.

"Have fun," said Joe as we paid him a handful of pesos. "Keep safe."

3

The Philippines is of course most famous for its tenth president, Ferdinand Marcos. With his wife, Imelda, the president had made international news in the 1980s because of his corruption and despot-like nature. This eventually led to his downfall, but during his twenty years in power, rumours abounded that the couple had managed to embezzle billions of dollars into overseas accounts.

I remember watching TV as a teenager, all about Imelda Marcos's stash of mink coats, gowns, handbags and shoes. She had thousands of pairs. It was both amazing and disgusting to see them. From then on, every time my mother bought herself a new pair of shoes, my dad's comment was always, 'Who do you think you are? Imelda Marcos?'

After depositing our suitcase in our room, Angela and I decided to venture out into the immediate vicinity. The sun was going down, but there was enough light so that we'd be able to see into the shadows. We handed the key to the receptionist and headed for the door.

Outside, we stepped past the armed guard, and almost immediately, a flurry of taxi drivers shouted for our attention. We waved them all away. Instead, we crossed a busy main road next to the US embassy, and then turned along a street leading to the sea front.

"What do you think of Manila so far?" I asked Angela.

"It's got a bit of an edge."

She was right. Even though no one was bothering us, a few people were staring. Involuntarily, I put my hand over my pocket, checking for the safety of my wallet. "Dollar! Dollar!" said a child's voice from behind. A filthy boy aged about seven was running up to us. He was wearing a dirty white T-shirt and little else. "Dollar for food!" he wailed. I shook my head but he followed, jumping in front of us, holding out his hand.

"No," I said firmly.

"*Please!*"

"No."

We walked on, and the boy didn't follow. It felt cruel not to give him anything, but if we had done so, we'd have been surrounded in minutes.

The palm-fringed promenade we'd seen from the car earlier smelled like a festering urinal. The beach, if you could call it that, was the resting place for sewage outflow. It was disgusting. Angela was pulling a face and trying to cover her nose.

"Let's go back," I said. "It's getting dark, anyway."

As we returned to the hotel, we passed a few dimly-lit side streets. In the shadows, slumbering homeless people and begging children loitered. Along another street was a brightly lit 7-Eleven store, with a congregation of unfortunates outside. Like almost all other businesses in the area, it had an armed guard standing by the entrance. We were glad when we reached the safety of our hotel and its armed guard.

4

The next morning was sunny, but horrendously humid. After a coffee in Starbucks, we walked to Rizal Park. Along the short way, three beggars approached us, all of them small children, all of them demanding money.

The park was named after Jose Rizal, a 19th century revolutionary leader and national hero of the Philippines. It was Rizal, many say, who sowed the seeds for independence from the Spanish. In the end, though, Filipino soldiers (under the jurisdiction of the Spanish Army) executed him by firing squad. The spot where this happened was inside the park.

Just past the entrance was a parade of Filipino flags that led to the Rizal Monument, a large bronze and granite obelisk, which also featured a sculpture of the great man. At the base of the monument, a couple of guards were standing to attention. Nearby was a small placard. It showed the exact spot where Rizal was shot.

"What are they all doing?" asked Angela as we moved further into the green park. In the middle of a grassy area were about twenty teenagers. All of them wore black trousers and ripped white

T-shirts. One of them had a large Filipino flag on the end of a long pole. They seemed to be involved in some sort of drama or dance activity, because, as we watched, they began chanting together, then springing forward and pretending to fall over. Then they would repeat the whole thing.

"Jesus, I'm hot," I said as sweat dribbled down my back. "Let's head for the fort before I drop dead."

5

"I would give Manila a 'C plus'," I said to Angela.

Angela looked around, taking note of things in the vicinity. She glanced at the traffic, and then at the pavements. "Yeah, I'd agree with that." We were grading Manila based on my very unscientific *Index of Development Scale*.

My scale classifies countries into four broad bands, A to D, with Class A countries (such as Japan, USA and Australia) being the richest, and Class D countries being the poorest. The index is based on five key things: coils, paths, roads, banknotes, and finally, homelessness. As we wandered towards the old Spanish fort, I looked around for more evidence to back up my 'C' grade.

Coils of electrical cables and wires (usually amassed on poles at street intersections) were a good indicator of how rich a nation was. Manila had lots of them hanging all over the place, similar to the coils we'd seen in Phnom Penh and some places in Africa. The more dense and loose the coils, the lower the country went on my scale.

Paths were another gauge of the state of a nation. In Tokyo, the pavements and sidewalks had been pristine, but in Manila, they were chipped and broken, and in some cases missing altogether. Absent manhole covers and deep, stagnant drains added to the effect. But at least Manila had pavements, I thought. Some places we'd been to hadn't.

When thinking about roads, I wasn't so much looking at the state of the actual tarmac, but rather the lane discipline drivers kept. In the UK and America, traffic was usually orderly, and the same could be said about Taipei and Tokyo. But in Manila, the roads were clogged with smoke-spewing trucks and jeepneys, all of which ignored basic lane discipline. A two-lane road in downtown Manila often meant a honking mess of vehicles three or four abreast.

The physical state of a country's banknotes was another indicator as to how well it was doing. In Hong Kong, Bangkok, Tokyo, and even Vietnam, the banknotes had been fine. None were blackened with grime, or bandaged together with tape. None drooped pathetically when held at one end. But in Manila, my wallet was stuffed with such things.

But perhaps the biggest measure of a country's wealth is the number of homeless people. Manila was full of people lounging by the side of streets, sleeping on filthy bits of cardboard or lying on dirty sheets. We passed one such family lying on the pavement. A woman had a girl on her lap, and was rummaging about in her hair. Dad was asleep behind them, as was the teenage son, swinging on a hammock tied between a fence and a tree trunk. All around them were piles of litter. When the girl saw us approaching, she jumped off her mother's lap and ran straight to us.

"Peso! Peso!" she shouted. "Peso!"

As we had with all the other beggars we had come across, we waved the girl away, and continued towards the fortress entrance.

6

Intramuros, at its peak in the 16th century, had been a formidable walled city, containing stately homes, government buildings, schools and churches, and indeed everything the Spanish needed to protect their interests. Like a plot from a movie, the fortress survived pirate attacks and sieges, but was then almost destroyed in the last stages of World War II. The Battle of Manila saw some of the fiercest fighting between US, Filipino and Japanese troops; in the midst of the battles, 100,000 Filipino civilians died. All that remained of the original fort was the surrounding walls and a few buildings.

Before Angela and I entered the complex, we decided to grab a drink from a nearby 7-Eleven store. Inside, we witnessed a daring heist. The culprit, a young man carrying a sack over his shoulder, was clearly homeless. His bedraggled appearance, together with his feverish eyes, gave him the look of a desperado. In full view of the five or six people in the shop, he stumbled straight for the aisle selling crisps and nuts. Once there, he began filling his sack.

The girl behind the counter noticed him straight away and starting yelling. The thief ignored her and continued to grab furious handfuls of snacks. Leaving the counter, the girl ran towards the man, shouting for the security guard outside to help apprehend the thief. The guard didn't hear her, and continued his conversation with a woman he seemed to know. Undeterred, the girl (half the size of the thief) began attacking the man, grabbing at his bag and pulling his hair. Instead of fighting back, the thief pushed her out of the way and lurched for the exit with his sack of goodies. The girl chased him. She was like a terrier. Everyone trooped outside to see what would happen next.

Both thief and shop assistant were gone. The security guard had ceased his conversation, and, like the rest of us, was staring along the street. Some help he'd been, I thought. We all stood for a moment wondering what to do. And then the girl came back around the corner. She was breathing heavily and her hair was all over the place. In her arms, she carried bags of crisps and nuts.

7

"I can't believe she did that," said Angela as we entered the old Spanish fort.

"No," I said agreeing. "And that security guard wasn't much help. *She* should be a security guard."

We walked to Manila Cathedral, staring up at the green domes. I'd heard that the Filipinos were fiercely religious, and could see for myself how true it was. Groups of smartly-dressed schoolchildren were walking through the entrance, worksheets at the ready, excited looks on their faces. All of them made the Sign of the Cross as they passed over the threshold.

But the main draw of the Intramuros complex was Fort Santiago, an area of old walls, bastions and dungeons. Jose Rizal had spent his last days in one of the dungeons, and we were hoping to find his cell. We walked through some gates into an area of cafes and trees.

We came to a large stone gate near a lily pond. A heron was at one end of the pond, beak poised as it studied the water; it was as still as a statue.

The gate was in the middle of a tall stone wall, blackened from the traffic fumes outside. We walked through it, following a well-trodden path around the ruins, occasionally stopping at cannons or sections of old buildings. Finally, we found the part of Fort Santiago where Rizal had been imprisoned. A group of camera-toting teenagers had arrived before us at the cell, and so we read the placard on the wall. It said that Jose Rizal had been held in the cell between 3rd November and 29th December 1896. His cell, when we finally saw it, was roped off and bare. There was nothing inside apart from some cream-coloured walls.

Back outside again, we climbed a battlement, which offered a good view of the Pasig River. Belching smoke came from the tugboats, of which there were many, and on the other side of the wide brown river, we could see some shack-type dwellings. The river didn't look particularly inviting; since the 1990s, the river had been declared biologically dead. We took a few photos and climbed back down.

8

With the heat and humidity becoming unbearable, we headed to a cafe we'd spotted earlier. As Angela sat down, I noticed a colourful gecko on a nearby wall. While I took a photo, Angela told me that the sweat patch had reappeared on my trousers. I felt my rear and touched dampness. Even my back was slick. "It looks like you've wet yourself again," said Angela.

"Thanks."

"I'm just telling you."

When our drinks arrived, I came up with a plan of action. In my mind, it would be a simple but highly effective way of disguising the unsightly patch. Making sure that no one was watching, I poured half of my water over the front of my trousers. The chill the liquid offered was amazing.

"What are you doing?" barked Angela, eyes incredulous.

"What do you think I'm doing?"

"I have no idea."

"It's so that people will think I've spilled a drink on me, and not realise that I'm actually a sweaty bastard."

Angela looked at the massive wet patch on the front of my trousers now. "No they won't. They'll think you've wet yourself even more now. I can't believe you did that. What were you thinking?"

Angela was right. It was an insane idea. I stared at my new wet patch. It looked like I was incontinent. We had to sit for a long while until the dampness started to evaporate.

9

Later that afternoon, we decided to visit Greenhills Shopping Centre, a place that specialised in fake clothing and pirated DVDs.

We caught a cab driven by Albert, a jovial man in his fifties. He told us he'd been a taxi driver for twenty-five years, and his job had provided him with enough money to raise his three daughters.

"One is the manager of KFC here in Manila, and the middle one is an accountant," he told us proudly. "My youngest daughter does not work – she has Down's syndrome. I recently bought her a computer, which she loves. She plays games all the time, especially something called *Farmville*. And do you know what? Those games really help her. She looks happy. But it has been hard for her since my wife died of cancer in 2007."

We came to a horrendous traffic jam. Men walked up and down the lines of stationary vehicles selling bottles of water, feather dusters, and quite strangely, fishing rods. While waiting for things to clear, Albert asked us if we were fans of Suzie Boyle.

"*Susan* Boyle? The singer?" I said, referring to the woman who had once appeared on a TV talent show.

"Yes. Suzie Boyle. From Ireland. You've heard of her?"

"Yes. She's very famous." I didn't think it was worth pointing out that Boyle was actually from Scotland.

"I love that lady's voice," he told us. "She reminds me of Barbra Streisand."

Our taxi shuffled forward a few metres. "Look!" Albert said. He was pointing at a fruit and vegetable stall. It was on the intersection, jutting out into the road, blocking a whole lane of traffic. "That is the cause of this jam! And it is a sign of the corruption in Manila. The vendor running the stall has paid the police to leave him alone. A hundred peso stuffed into someone's back pocket. But traffic problems are the result."

To escape the jam, Albert took us on a shortcut filled with shack-like homes. "The people who live here go to sleep in the open air. Sometimes, in the night, rats will run over their bellies. Sometimes they will bite people's toes. This is no joke."

But despite his comments, Albert was still clearly proud of his city. "Yes, there are many homeless people in Manila. But mostly, they are happy and not going without food. Our homeless people are not like the people in Sudan. The Philippines is not a Third World country! We have malls, we have electricity, and we have flash cars. I often tell my daughters how lucky they are to live here."

Five minutes later, we arrived at Greenhills Shopping Centre.

10

The shopping centre was a vast, multi-storey mall filled with people and cheap goods. In one of the upper levels, stalls only sold mobile phones and MP3 players. Neither of us had seen so much technology in any one place. Even compared to the gadget stores of Tokyo, it was unbelievable.

"Welcome, Sir! Welcome, Ma'am!" was a cry we heard over and over as we wandered the aisles, and then, from out of nowhere a young man wearing a white T-shirt approached me. "You want DVD?" he whispered, eyes shifting from side to side, looking around and over us. He was like a meerkat.

I nodded.

"Follow me."

The man led us through a maze of aisles, turning left and then right, before taking a shortcut through a dense clothing section. We reached some stairs and went down them; the man scouting the area as we did so. It seemed a strange way of going about business, I thought, because as far as we were aware, the shopping centre was famous for its pirate DVDs. And with the amount of crime outside, the police were hardly going to concern themselves over some knockoff movies. But the way the young man was carrying on, it was as if we were trying to buy cocaine.

Eventually, we arrived at a quieter section of the shopping centre, and the shifty man led us to a tiny store. Inside was a range of hi-fi equipment and portable TVs. There was no sign of any DVDs at all. After peeping through the window to check we hadn't been followed, the man gave a nod to another man behind the counter. Then, like a speakeasy, a thick wad of DVDs appeared on the counter, as did a book. It was a master list of movies they had available.

We eventually bartered the owner down from his initial asking price of 4500 pesos (about £65) to 2200 pesos for our booty of DVDs. They were bundled together and wrapped up in plain paper. Finally, they were put inside a simple plastic bag. We left the store and headed outside, the master criminals that we were.

11

"Welcome to Manila!" our friend Andrew said later that evening. We met him outside Starbucks in the Makati district of the city. It was a part of Manila full of modern skyscrapers, upmarket malls and posh restaurants. There was not a beggar to be seen. The 'C plus' grade we'd given Manila earlier looked wrong. We were in a definite 'A' list part of the city. It was like Hong Kong or Bangkok.

"Thanks," I said, pumping his hand. Andrew looked well, and was healthily tanned. Moving to the Philippines had done him the world of good. Back in the UK, he'd been deathly pale and gaunt-looking.

Andrew led us to a bar, and the three of us started chatting about life in the Philippines. "When I first got here, I really wasn't sure," Andrew admitted. "The heat, the humidity, and the pollution, not to mention starting a new a job in a strange country – it all got to me. Initially I felt I didn't really want to be here, but bit by bit, things got easier. I got used to the heat, I started to enjoy my job, and I made new friends. So yeah, I've warmed to the place."

"Aren't you worried, though?" asked Angela. "I mean, about all the crime."

Andrew nodded. "Yeah, I know Manila has a reputation for violent crime, but all I can say is that I haven't seen anything myself, at least so far. And I don't know anyone else who has either."

Because Andrew was a single Western man in Manila, it didn't take long for the conversation to move onto the topic of Filipino women. We had already seen a few older Western men with young local women in Manila.

"If I wanted a Filipino girlfriend," Andrew said. "I could get one just like that." He snapped his fingers for effect. "It's because I have money, and that's attractive to some women over here. That's why you see these older guys with young locals. But it's the same in Thailand and Vietnam."

"So you haven't got a girlfriend over here?" I asked.

Andrew shook his head. "I'll tell you what worries me – it's whether any potential girlfriend would genuinely like me, or whether it's just my wallet she likes. It makes you paranoid."

I think I understood what he meant.

"Right," Andrew said. "I'll get us some more drinks."

12

I decided I needed the toilet, and so, after getting directions from Andrew I went to find them. When I entered the small, dark room, I discovered a single cubicle without a door. There wasn't even a urinal or sink. So, with a bursting bladder, I lifted the toilet seat, and wished I hadn't. A ghastly, indescribable sight assaulted my vision. It looked like someone had voided their entire innards into the bowl. It was disgusting, and smelled so rancid that it made me want to vomit. I tried to flush the mess away, but the mechanism was broken, and it was at that point that another man entered the toilet room. One of my hands was on the flush, the other on the toilet seat.

"It's not working," I mumbled, even though I knew what the man was thinking. I hurried out of the toilet, back into the sanctuary of the bar.

"I'll take you to another bar close to here," said Andrew. "The toilets there will be fine."

He led us outside onto a street covered with red neon signs. "I call this the Street of Shame. It's full of girlie bars and massage parlours." One large sign showed a montage of pretty girls' faces with the slogan: The Sexiest Girls Await Your Pleasure!

The Heckle and Jeckle bar was evidently a popular place for the ex-pats of Manila, mainly due to the large TV screens showing live sport. The pool tables were also crowded. After I'd rushed to the toilets (thankfully clean), I joined Andrew and Angela at the table.

"I still can't believe you came to Manila," said Andrew, taking a photo of us. His camera flashed, causing my eyes to scrunch up. The resulting image had us laughing for a good few minutes.

"I told you we would," I answered.

"So where are you going next?"

"Kuala Lumpur," Angela said. "And then Borneo to see the orang-utans. I can't wait for that."

"Wow."

"I know," I said. "We are lucky."

A couple of hours later, it was time to say goodbye to our friend. Angela and I had an early flight the next morning.

"Well, if you're ever back in Manila," said Andrew, "you know where to find me."

We shook hands and bid him fond farewell. After pointing us in the right direction to get a taxi, we said goodbye again. "And thanks for coming," he said. "I just hope you go away with a decent impression of the Philippines. It's not all gun crime and beggars. There are some gorgeous unspoilt beaches and some great little mountain towns. And I don't know whether you've noticed or not, but the Filipino people are some of the friendliest you'll ever meet. They really make you feel at home."

We shook hands and climbed in the taxi.

Chapter 12: Kuala Lumpur, capital of Malaysia

The two words making up the name of the Malaysian capital seemed to roll off my tongue in the most pleasing way possible. The four syllables conjured up images of the tropics, of skyscrapers, of Asia. It didn't matter that the actual Malay translation of Kuala Lumpur was actually 'muddy river junction'; it still sounded good to me

"How many countries have we been to so far?" asked Angela as we waited for a taxi outside Kuala Lumpur International airport terminal. It was good to be back in a Class 'A' country after the grime and fumes of the Philippines, even if the humidity was actually worse.

"Well, if we say that Hong Kong and Macau count as China, this is our eighth country, nine if we count Taiwan."

"That's amazing."

"I know. And we've still got Indonesia to go."

A taxi pulled up and we got in.

2

We regarded the scenery outside. The highway was of exceptional quality, and beyond it was a landscape of palm tree jungle. The cars along the highway seemed in good condition too, with none of the tuk-tuks, jeepneys or dilapidated trucks that many Southeast Asian countries seemed to have in abundance.

As we approached the outskirts of the city, newly-built residential areas were everywhere, homes for rich city workers, and then through the haze, we could make out the skyscrapers of downtown Kuala Lumpur.

"The weather is not so good," said the taxi driver. "Forest fires cause much pollution over the city. The smoke blows over from Indonesia. But at least the rain has stopped." Forty-five minutes later, we pulled up outside our hotel. After paying the driver and unpacking our things, we hit the streets of downtown Kuala Lumpur.

A few things struck us immediately. Firstly, there was no litter. And I mean no litter. The roads and paths were all squeaky clean, clinically so. If someone from Phnom Penh or Manila could see what the streets of KL (to give it its shortened form) were like, they would not believe it. The other thing we noticed was the quietness of the traffic. Unlike Hanoi, or even Bangkok, the road system in Kuala Lumpur, though busy, was a civilised affair. There was no honking or death-defying lane swerving; instead, drivers made their way around the city in a sensible and orderly fashion.

The people wandering around were a cosmopolitan bunch too. As well as the local Malays, there were young backpackers and older travellers (perhaps stopping off en-route to Australia), as well as people from India, Japan and Africa. All of them gave the streets a truly international feel. Neon-lit restaurants and bars were everywhere, as were malls selling luxury items. Towering above it all were the skyscrapers, including the twin Petronas Towers.

"We'll visit them tomorrow," I said. "Today I just want to relax by the pool."

3

The next morning, Angela and I were up early to see the sights. When we stepped outside, we caught sight of the street cleaners putting their final touches to the sidewalks and roads. Some were even washing the pavements with mops and buckets.

Our guidebook suggested the best time to visit the Petronas Towers was early in the morning. We arrived ten minutes after opening time, at 8.40am, and found ourselves at the back of a massive queue. Resigning ourselves to a long and arduous wait, we shuffled forward as more and more people joined from behind.

"Why do you hate queuing so much?" Angela asked after I'd moaned for the tenth time.

"Because it's a waste of time. We could be out seeing things, but instead we're cooped up in here."

"But everyone has to queue."

"Presidents and kings don't."

"No, and neither do people who think ahead and buy their tickets online. I can't believe we didn't do that."

Thirty minutes later, one of the men in charge of tickets walked down the line of people. He was carrying a small sign saying, No More Tickets For Afternoon Viewing. As he made his way along, he was counting people's heads, working out where the last ticket would be. As he got closer to us, I dared him to stop. *Go on*, I silently thought. *Just you bloody dare! And then you'll know what queue rage is.*

The man slowed and counted a few more heads. Then he looked at Angela and me, and stopped counting. He walked towards us, but then carried on past, stopping a few feet behind. With an apology to the people who had just missed out, he dropped his little sign and told them they could continue queuing for the evening slots, or try again the next morning. If we'd arrived one minute later, we would've been on the other side of his sign. I looked at the people behind us. They looked shocked and uncomprehending, but most of them stayed in the queue.

Fifteen minutes later, we arrived at the ticket counter and gratefully received our passes. Our tickets told us our slot was for later that afternoon (the morning ones had long gone), and so with time on our hands, we ventured outside to find the nearest monorail station.

The train deposited us at Merdeka Square, a large expanse of green surrounded by a set of colonial buildings dating back to British rule. Perhaps the grandest of all was the Sultan Abdul Samad Building, a large domed affair designed by a Brit and initially used as an administrative building. Today it is a Malaysian court of law. Across from it was one of the highest flagpoles in the world. At the top, a huge but limp Malaysian flag sagged pathetically, unable to fly due to the lack of wind.

"Shall we go for a fish massage?" I asked.

"I'm not sure," replied Angela. "I don't know whether I'll like it."

"You won't know if you don't try."

4

Earmarked for demolition at one point, the Central Market was a small but thriving shopping centre. Unlike the larger malls of Kuala Lumpur that catered for international brands, the Central Market was full of boutique shops selling local silks, artwork and lotions. After a cursory browse through some of them, we entered the fish massage emporium.

"I don't like it!" cried Angela five minutes later. She had just dipped her feet into a small tank filled with tiny darting fish. Her face smiled, grimaced, and then laughed, all in the space of two seconds. "It's weird! And so ticklish!"

My feet went in and were soon swarming with toothless fish, all sucking at some part of my toes, heels and ankles. Like Angela had said, it was extremely ticklish, and a little bit unnerving too. And this was only the nursery pool, populated by tiddlers; behind us was a much larger tank filled with hundreds of bigger fish. It was time to move on to the big boys.

Angela went first, and forty or fifty fish immediately surrounded her feet. She grimaced and laughed in equal measure, her eyes going wide and then closing again, which brought a smile from the lady in charge. These bigger fish seemed hungrier and looked like they had a lot more *suck* to them. I stuck my feet in and they came like piranhas. It was the strangest sensation I'd ever experienced, and I could barely stand it. It was as if a hundred feathers were tickling my feet at the same time.

Afterwards, walking away from the fish spa, we both agreed it had been well worth the effort in finding it.

5

"You look like Wayne Wooney!" said our taxi driver as we headed towards the Perdana Botanical Gardens.

I'd noticed the man staring at me from his rear-view mirror. But if he thought I looked like Wayne Rooney, then perhaps he needed his eyes checked. I was fourteen years older than the Manchester United footballer was, for a start. Plus he had much more hair since getting his implants.

"I don't think so," I replied.

"But you a famous footballer, yes?" It seemed a genuine question, which caused even more hilarity from Angela.

During colonial times, the British elite had built their homes in the gardens. Nowadays, though, the Perdana Botanical Gardens' main draw is its bird park. It promised a wide variety of indigenous birds, all housed within a gigantic net sprawled between lofty pylons. We paid the fee and entered.

"This isn't what I expected," I said to Angela as we arrived at a cage with an owl perched inside. "I thought the birds would be free, not locked up."

Angela nodded, looking at the miserable owl inside the enclosure. It looked like it didn't have much room to do anything, let alone fly. Owls weren't the only birds trapped inside cages: hawks, emus, ostriches, and hornbills were also under lock and key. But some of these I could perhaps understand. The beak on the hornbill looked strong enough to crack a human skull. But why were budgies kept in cages? What were they going to do: tweet someone to death?

Plenty of birds could fly free, though. Peacocks, storks, flamingos, exotic pigeons and brightly coloured finches were everywhere, some of them swooping low over our heads. One lazy stork landed on a pathway in front of us, and then flopped to the ground, resting on its rear with its spindly legs sprawled out in front.

We arrived at a signpost, which offered warnings and rules. Please Do Not Feed the Birds, was one sensible one, as was, Please Don't Shout At The Birds. But the one I was most taken with was the one saying, Please Do Not Pull the Birds' Feathers.

After a walk around a large pond filled with flamingos, and then a quick drink in the Hornbill Restaurant, we headed back outside. It was time to get some lunch.

6

"I've been thinking," I said, using my spoon to scoop up some noodles. "While we're in Borneo, we should visit Brunei."

Angela looked up from her bowl of chicken and fried noodles. So far, Malaysia's culinary delights had been mundane compared to the delicacies of Taiwan and Cambodia. And for that, we were thankful. "Brunei?"

"Yeah. I've been checking it out. We can get a cheap return flight from Kota Kinabalu to Brunei – it only takes half an hour. We can have a day trip there. What do you think?"

Angela shrugged. "Are you sure we can do it in one day? Because if going to Brunei means we won't have time to see the orang-utans, then I don't want to go."

"No, it won't interfere with that. The only issue is that it's one day fewer to relax by the pool. But we can do that this afternoon at our hotel. We've got hours before we go to the Petronas Towers."

Angela twisted a line of noodles inside her spoon. "Okay."

7

To be honest, the trip to the viewing platform of the world's tallest twin towers was not worth the hassle. For a start, we had to wait thirty minutes before we were allowed inside the elevator. And then, when we got in, a man wearing a security badge told us we could only stay at the Petronas Towers viewing platform for ten minutes.

"Anyone who takes longer than ten minutes," he said, "will be shot."

Actually, he hadn't said that at all.

The viewing platform was about half way to the top, and was actually part of the sky bridge that connected both towers. As the doors opened, the man in charge reminded us again of the time constraint, and then allowed us out. We all spread out along the walkway, snapping photos of the world below us.

"I think the view from our hotel is better," said Angela, and I nodded in agreement.

"So what shall we do now?" I asked.

"How about that cave thing you showed me in the book earlier? The one with the giant golden statue?"

"Yeah, good idea. Ten minutes is actually just enough time to stay up here, isn't it?"

8

Batu Caves were located north of the city centre. When we arrived, the sight of an enormous 140-foot golden statue guarding the caves greeted us. It was of a Hindu god called Lord Murugan, and the temple he was guarding attracted over 1.5 million pilgrims every year. It was one of the most popular Hindu shrines outside India.

There were quite a few tourists, most of them on the massive staircase behind the statue. But apart from people, the temple had two other things in great abundance: monkeys and litter. Monkeys were everywhere. They were scurrying across the temple steps or crawling along the high walls by the entrance. Some were eating bits of banana and others were simply sitting around looking bored. The amount of litter was off-putting though; it was all over the place, on the steps, around the statue and piled up by the walls.

Compared to central Kuala Lumpur, the Batu Caves complex was a rubbish tip.

"This way for tickets!" said a smiling man approaching us. "Two tickets is thirty ringgit!"

I handed over the cash, which was worth £6; in return, the man gave us a pair of wristbands. Thanking him, we headed for the base of the 273 steps, but the man shouted for our attention. "No, this way." He was gesturing towards a narrow bridge crossing over a carp-filled pool. A sign near the bridge said, Cave Villa. Clearly, we'd paid to see something else.

Slightly irked, we made our way across the bridge. Inside the cave entrance was a collection of Hindu sculptures and artwork. After a cursory glance at them, we carried on further inside, until we arrived at a reptile enclosure. Snakes, lizards and turtles were all contained inside tiny tanks. We were the only people there, apart from a bored teenager with a magazine. He looked up briefly to check we had our wristbands on, and then carried on reading.

"This is awful," whispered Angela, staring into a tank containing two small turtles. One of them was dead, the other, barely alive.

We didn't linger long inside the Cave Villa after that.

9

Soon we were climbing the steps towards the Cave Temple. It had been free to enter all along. At one point, we passed a strange statue of a mythical animal. It had a man's head, a peacock's tail, a cow's body, some bull's horns and, strangest of all, a pair of pert breasts on the front.

At the top of the steps, we staggered into a huge cavern. Winged things flew from one cliff face to another. But these were not bats, they were pigeons, and they weren't the only birds in attendance. Numerous hens and roosters scuttled about on the cave floor. Suddenly, one of them crowed a horribly discordant call. It reverberated around the cave like something from a horror film.

Further into the cave, we came across a small temple, which was flanked on all sides by sheer cliff faces. Monkeys clambered over the rocks, and some braver individuals ran across the floor. One noticed a discarded can of cola and went to investigate. After discovering it was empty, the primate rolled it away, sending it tumbling down the steps.

"What a shame it's so dirty," said Angela. "This place could be amazing."

We walked to a stall selling tacky souvenir items. As well as small statues of the golden god outside, the stall sold A4-sized electronic pictures, the type that when plugged in, offered a light spectacle behind whatever the picture was. The last time I'd seen such a thing was in the 1970s.

"I think we should buy one," I said, "as a souvenir."

Angela looked unconvinced.

"No one has these any more. They're retro."

Most of the pictures showed Hindu deities, or scenes from Batu Caves, and each one was connected to a power supply to provide an electronic feast for the eyes. Golden rainbows, silver spirals, and multi-coloured raindrops made up the majority of backdrops, and they all looked tacky to the extreme. Accompanying the visual extravaganza was some tinny Indian music blaring from a couple of cheap speakers.

"I'm buying one," I announced, spying a particularly exciting picture of the golden statue. Instead of a cave and some steps, the background was aquamarine with a sparkly silver wheel in the middle. The spokes of the wheel offered the moving light show. It was the tackiest of the bunch.

After pointing it out to the proprietor, he nodded and disappeared behind his stall. When he reappeared, he passed me one already boxed up.

"Can you plug it in?" I asked. The last thing I wanted was a picture that didn't work.

The man nodded and removed the picture from its box. He soon located an empty socket on his already dangerously overloaded extension cable, and plugged it in.

Two things happened simultaneously. First, the music ceased, and second, the lights went out. Not just the lights on our particular picture, but also all the lights of the stall and, in fact, the immediate vicinity. The silence was unreal and the darkness startling. From somewhere a cock crowed.

In the end, the man gave us the picture that had been on display, and we clambered down the steps and back into a taxi.

10

"I'm not having it in the house," said Angela that evening. We were sitting in an outside bar enjoying a drink. It was our final night in the Malaysian capital before flying to Borneo the next day.

"You don't have to. I'm going to buy a long extension lead and put it in the garden. Our neighbours will be jealous."

Angela picked up her wine glass and spun it around a few times. The neon lights of downtown Kuala Lumpur reflected from it. I looked up at the Petronas Towers, glimmering in the black sky. The number of lights it had was amazing. I wondered how much it cost to power them. But when the owner was Petronas Petrochemicals, money was probably not a concern.

"I'm getting tired now," said Angela, putting her glass back on the table. "Not just tonight, but generally. We've hardly stopped on this trip. The last time we had a proper rest was in Phuket."

"I'm tired too. But we're staying in a nice hotel in Borneo. It has a beach and a nice pool. We can have a holiday from our holiday. Tomorrow can be a day of relaxation."

Angela smiled. "That does sound nice."

An hour later, we were packing our bags yet again.

Chapter 13. The Orang-utans of Borneo

Before arriving in Borneo, both Angela and I had imagined the island to be a place of unspoilt rainforest, of steamy jungles, of headhunters and of wild, exotic creatures. That illusion disappeared as we drove away from the airport.

There was no rainforest, only large expanses of palm trees – the palm oil they were producing was a valuable commodity for the island. The problem with this, however, was that the palms were replacing the indigenous rainforest, and therefore, the animals.

We passed people sitting at roadside stalls peddling fruit and vegetables. Others were sitting in ramshackle cafes, shaded from the sun underneath corrugated metal awnings. Some homes were little more than wooden shacks, quite often built on stilts. Nobody looked like a headhunter.

Borneo is actually the third largest island in the world, and three countries share it: Indonesia, Malaysia and Brunei. Indonesia has the largest chunk: the bottom two thirds of the island. Malaysia has most of the remainder, and tiny Brunei gets by with a minuscule section at the top. Our hotel was in the city of Kota Kinabalu, in the Malaysian section.

As we drove onwards, large billboards advertised luxury apartments and electronic tablets, and then we arrived on the outskirts of Kota Kinabalu, where finally, the palm forests receded.

"Okay," said the taxi driver. "Hotel not far. You lucky people! Is very nice hotel."

2

The Rasa Ria Shangri-La Hotel was opulence to the extreme. It had its own private golf course and its own private beach. We'd decided to splash out on this particular hotel because we were only going to be in Borneo for three days, and the Rasa Ria had an adjoining orang-utan rehabilitation centre. Guests of the hotel had first pick of visiting slots. After dumping our things in our room, we wasted no time in securing ourselves a viewing for the following morning. That done, we lounged by the pool, recharging our batteries for a few hours.

That evening, while wandering along an outdoor walkway within the hotel complex, we came across something lying in our path. At first, we thought it was a leaf, but upon closer inspection, it revealed itself to be a bat.

"Is it dead?" asked Angela, peering down to look. It was lying still, with its wings outstretched.

"I'm not sure." I carefully picked it up, and as I did so, it opened its mouth to reveal a tiny, but impressive, array of teeth. It wasn't trying to bite, it was just yawning. I placed the bat in a nearby plant pot, to get it out of harm's way. We were both surprised when the mammal immediately clambered out and flew away into the night.

Because the Rasa Ria was located some distance away from Kota Kinabalu town, we had no choice but to suffer the horrendous prices in the hotel restaurant. But the food was good, and the entertainment interesting. It involved a set of traditionally costumed people dancing with long poles of wood. When they started inviting guests to dance with them, Angela and I escaped to our room. We opened a beer each and sat on the balcony, watching as a gorgeous sunset spread out across the South China Sea.

3

The next morning, we made our way down to the orang-utan centre. With thirty or so other people, we watched a short DVD about the rehabilitation process for orang-utans.

The need for rehabilitation stemmed from the destruction of the rainforest, the natural habitat of the orang-utan. Angela and I were shocked to learn that over seventy percent of Malaysian rainforest in Borneo had been chopped down to make way for palm trees. Inevitably, the orang-utans were the losers in this game, with many young orang-utans becoming orphans in the process. That was why the rehabilitation centres had become so important in Borneo. They taught the young creatures how to look after themselves, how to forage and how to survive.

When the DVD ended, a ranger took hold of a microphone and addressed us. "There are five orang-utans at this rehabilitation centre. All of them are aged between three and five-years-old, and they are here for stage one of their rehabilitation. When they are ready, they will move to another centre for the next stage."

The ranger told us that there were four stages needed in the rehabilitation process. Stages two to four involved socialisation and independence, slowly getting the orang-utans used to less human interaction. "By the final stage," he said, "the orang-utans are able to build their own nests and find their own food. After long periods of observation, the creatures will be released into the wild."

Sepilok is the most famous orang-utan centre in Borneo, and is one of its top tourist destinations. Instead of just a handful of the creatures, Sepilok has between 60 and 80 of them. The orang-utans at the Kota Kinabalu rehabilitation centre would all eventually end up there.

"Okay," said the ranger, "now we'll take a short walk into the forest. There is a viewing platform where hopefully you will see some of these beautiful creatures. Follow me, please."

4

The steep walk up the forest trail was only a short one, but I was still sweating like a pig when we arrived at the viewing platform. Everyone crowded together, cameras at the ready, while the ranger stood some distance away with a bucket full of fruit. The area around us was thick jungle. The sound of insect calls was everywhere.

"Please keep as quiet as you can," the ranger instructed, staring about into the trees. As a hush descended, he cupped his hands and shouted something into the forest, presumably to entice the orang-utans to come to feed. Silence followed, and so, after a moment, the ranger repeated his call.

Suddenly, there was a loud rustle of branches, and our collective sense of anticipation was turned up a notch. The ranger called again, and we all craned our heads towards the treetops, hoping to catch a glimpse, even a tiny one, of a precious ape. But there was nothing; only the occasional sound of snapping branches, then silence. The insects began their tune again.

The ranger did his strange call again, and once more, we could hear the distant sound of branches snapping.

"There!" someone in our group said, and we all swiveled our necks to catch our first sighting of an orang-utan. There it was, high up in the foliage, and then it was gone. I lowered my camera and rubbed my neck. Ten minutes later, some small children behind us were getting restless, crying and fidgeting. Another five minutes passed, and the only thing keeping us going was the odd snatch of ginger fur high up in the forest.

"They should have a small child on standby for situations like this," I whispered to Angela. "Get him into the orange suit and make him run through the undergrowth, making monkey sounds."

Angela glared at me.

The ranger, maybe sensing our disappointment, came over and explained that perhaps the orang-utans had seen a snake. "This might be why they do not want to come and feed." He sat on a nearby bench and placed the bucket next to him.

But then, incredibly, one child-sized orang-utan decided that the lure of fresh melon was greater than the risk of a serpent attack, because it quickly descended a tree trunk, swung Tarzan-like across a rope and ran to the ranger's bench. It grabbed one of his fruity temptations, and then quickly clambered up a tree and disappeared from sight. The whole encounter had lasted perhaps five seconds.

As well as the brave fruit-grabbing orang-utan, there were two others in attendance. They were high in the treetops, moving with great speed through the branches, or else hanging off them like trapeze artists. One of them snapped a large branch, which began to fall towards our heads. It flipped and turned but thankfully missed where we were all standing, causing much hilarity from everyone. Then the first orang-utan appeared again. Instead of doing a snatch and grab approach, it jumped into the ranger's arms and curled itself around him. It looked cute and baby-like.

The ranger produced a bottle of juice, from which the orang-utan greedily drank. The whole scene was amazing, more so when we remembered that these animals were essentially wild. When the infant ape had finished the bottle, it jumped away, climbing back up a tree. With the show over, we all made our way back down to the hotel grounds, happy with the whole experience.

"I really enjoyed that," said Angela, looking back at some of the photos she'd taken.

"Yeah, so did I."

5

We caught a taxi to Kota Kinabalu town. It was a modern city, with a smattering of skyscrapers. It also had lots of traffic clogging the streets. Its best feature was its location on the edge of the South China Sea. The beautiful azure water reminded us of the ocean colours we'd seen off the coast of Phuket. A huge statue of a swordfish stood overlooking it, and some colourful wooden fishing boats bobbed about in it.

During the Second World War, the British Army had blown up most of Kota Kinabalu (or Jesselton as it was called then) to stop it from falling into Japanese hands. After a campaign of serious aerial bombardment, only three buildings remained. One was the spindly white Atkinson Clock Tower, the oldest building in Kota Kinabalu. Angela and I spotted it on a hill. It looked like a forgotten outpost, because it was surrounded by dense green jungle. But someone was clearly looking after the tower; its clock was showing the correct time and its weather vane looked in good condition.

"Was it a lighthouse or something?" asked Angela.

I shook my head. "Not a lighthouse, more of a navigational aid to passing ships. It was built to honour Jesselton's first governor. He died of malaria, I think."

The busy Sunday Market was thronging with Chinese goods and Chinese people. We passed a food stall selling chicken feet. An old woman was actually buying a bag full of the tasty treats. Further along, we came to a small section of the market dedicated to the sale of live animals. Puppies, kittens, small rabbits, cute yellow chicks and baby ducklings were all cooped up inside wire cages. Nearby, some tortoises and turtles were lying at the bottom of dirty buckets. Some were reaching upwards with their tiny flippers, trying to taste freedom. Angela couldn't bear to look at them, and so we walked out the other side.

"Let's find somewhere to get a drink," I said.

6

"A latte and one small bottle of orange juice," I said to the young woman behind the counter. Angela had already sat down somewhere.

The woman smiled and nodded, and then set to work. A doughnut came first, which surprised me, because I hadn't ordered it. But I didn't get a chance to query the unwanted addition because the girl had already moved to the coffee machine. When she returned and put the latte and orange juice down on the tray, I gestured to the doughnut.

"No doughnut," I said. "I didn't order it."

The girl smiled and said the doughnut was free. She then passed me the bill. It made no mention of the doughnut, but did have an item called 'glacier' on it.

"Excuse me," I said. "What is glacier?" I pointed to the bill.

The waitress smiled and informed me that glacier meant doughnut.

"But I thought you said the doughnut was free?"

"Yes, doughnut free when you buy coffee!" she said, eyeing the other customers waiting behind me.

I sighed. "So if the doughnut is free, why have I been charged three ringgit?" I pointed at the bill again.

The girl looked at the bill, and then at the lonely doughnut, and seemed genuinely confused. "Doughnut free!" she said.

I admitted defeat, paid my money, and sat down with my doughnut and drinks.

7

That afternoon, instead of sitting on the beach, we booked ourselves on a cycling trip. For fifty ringgit each (£10) we were given a bike and a helmet. With eight other people, we set off on a gently paced ride towards a local village called Terayong. Along the way, we passed mangrove swamps (full of shy crabs that hid in their holes as we cycled by), and then some brightly coloured wooden houses. Small children sat in the shade near the houses, and chickens pecked in the dust. None seemed to mind our presence.

Our guide was a young man barely out of his teens. He told us that a lot of the hotel staff lived in the village. That was why no one minded us being there. "Please climb off your bicycles," he said. "And leave them here. They will be safe." We did so, and followed him to a small wooden jetty that jutted out into a wide brown river. At the far end of the jetty was a platform, constructed on stilts. We all congregated there, looking at the river and a small stilt village that had grown around a riverbank. In the distance was Mount Kinabalu.

"The people who live here mostly lead a simple life. Apart from the hotel workers, families survive by growing crops, but mostly by fishing and catching crabs from the river. As you can see, it is a very peaceful and beautiful place to live. I have lived here since I was born. My parents still live here, and my grandparents too. Come. We will ride to someone's house now. It belongs to a woman from the village. She has prepared some snacks for us to try."

We rode through the village, passing a small shop with some bare footed children playing outside. A few minutes later, we all dismounted near the woman's home, and our guide led us to a large outdoor table. A smiling woman appeared and brought each of us a plate of fried bananas, and then something else wrapped in leaves. It was clearly a rehearsed deal with the bicycle tour, but we didn't mind as we tucked in. Next, we all had a go at cooking a local pancake made with palm oil, and then to finish off, the woman poured us a small cup of coffee each. It was almost black, but palatable. The beans had been ground by the woman using a pestle and mortar.

Half an hour later, Angela and I were back at the hotel, lounging on the beach.

"So, tomorrow we go to Brunei," I said, slapping on another layer of suntan cream. There was no way I was having a repeat of the sunburn incident of Phuket. "And then the day after that, Bali."

Angela didn't say anything for a while. Eventually she looked up and smiled. "This is paradise."

Both of us closed our eyes. The only sound was the gentle crashing of waves from the South China Sea.

Chapter 14. The Sultanate of Brunei

"I hope you haven't got any bullets on you," I said to Angela as we came in to land at Brunei's rather small international airport. "Because if you have, you're done for. You're not even allowed to have them on a necklace."

I'd just been reading the information about entry requirements given to us by the cabin crew. Possession of a bullet in any shape, way or form was a serious offense in Brunei: the punishment was imprisonment, and at least three strokes with a cane. Possession of drugs was worse. On the back of our immigration card, in large red letters, it read: THE PENALTY FOR DRUGS IS DEATH.

The tiny Sultanate of Brunei (only about twice the size of Luxembourg) is located on the northern edge of Borneo, and its capital, Bandar Seri Begawan, was where we were heading. Brunei gained its independence from the UK in 1984, and the current ruler, Hassanal Bolkiah, is the 29th in a long line of royalty dating back to the fifteenth century.

The Sultan of Brunei is famously wealthy, and one of his follies is cars. He is rumoured to have over three thousand of them, worth an estimated $4 billion. This is a man who owns not one Rolls Royce, but five hundred! When he tires of his cars, he has his own private jet, a Boeing 747 with a gold-plated interior. He sometimes flies it himself.

There have been other memorable sultans. Take Abdul Momin (1852-1885), for instance. He was a man well known for his fairness and wisdom and, get this, his supernatural powers. What these 'powers' entailed, is a subject of mystery, but I'd wager it made him popular at parties. But the prize for most colourful ruler must go to the 22nd sultan, Muhammed Alam (1804-1804). For a start, he called himself the King of Fire, which didn't really bode well for his sanity, and he had a peculiar habit at mealtimes. He liked eating liver. But not ordinary liver: *children's liver!* His short reign ended when he was publicly garrotted, which, appropriately enough, was his own choice for execution.

2

When Angela and I had boarded our Royal Brunei Airlines flight in Kota Kinabalu, an announcement came over the PA informing us that a blessing would be made for the upcoming flight. A few moments later, a man's voice started singing a haunting melody in Arabic. Everyone sat and listened quietly.

When the singing ended, a well-spoken British accent came over the PA. "Hello, this is your captain speaking. I'd like to welcome you aboard this Royal Brunei Airbus A320. The short hop to Bandar Seri Begawan should take around twenty minutes, and we'll be flying on a southerly routing, reaching a cruising altitude of ten thousand feet."

The flight lasted twenty-two minutes, and we were soon on the ground. Customs was easy, and we wandered through to arrivals to meet our guide for the day, a local woman called Jesslyn. "Welcome to Brunei," she said, smiling.

Jesslyn led us to the air-conditioned 4x4 that would be our vehicle throughout the day. "Our first stop will be the Jame' Asr Hassanil Bolkiah Mosque," she told us as we fastened our seatbelts. "It was commissioned by the current sultan in 1994."

Bandar Seri Begawan seemed extremely clean and well ordered. There was not a scrap of rubbish anywhere. Also, the traffic was light, at least for a capital city. And the cars looked expensive. But the thing we noticed most were the images of the smiling sultan.

They were on billboards, on the front of shops and even on a gateway to a timber yard. Some enormous posters of the man also adorned a set of tall buildings. In them, the sultan was wearing a pristine white uniform and cap; his chest covered in medals. The number of images seemed overkill.

"It was our king's birthday ten days ago," explained Jesslyn. "That is why his picture is everywhere. Also, everyone had to put flags up outside their homes."

"Had to?"

"Yes. A message was put on television asking everyone to show the flags and...well...everyone did."

3

Brunei's wealth comes from oil, a fact that probably saved the country from being taken over by neighbouring Malaysia.

Sultan Haji Omar Ah Saifuddien III (the current ruler's father) came to the throne in 1950, and used the money to transform Brunei from a dull backwater into a thriving nation. A fair proportion of the wealth went directly to the sultan himself, which has since passed down to his son; but with so much money coming into the country's coffers, a lot of it went to the people too. Everyone in Brunei receives free education and health care. No one pays any tax. There is no poverty, and everyone seems happy with this arrangement.

The sultan is obviously a well-liked and popular man in Brunei, unlike his younger brother, Prince Jefri. The prince had been the country's finance minister, and it hadn't taken him long to start embezzling funds – millions of dollars by all accounts. Instead of keeping his indiscretion under wraps, and perhaps whisking the money away to overseas accounts to be spent at a later date, the prince bought two thousand cars and a collection of gold-plated toilet brushes. He then purchased a gigantic yacht, which he named *Tits*. It came with two lifeboats that he called *Nipple 1* and *Nipple 2*. When his brother found out about this extravagance (and he was no slouch himself when it came to excessiveness), the Sultan sacked the prince from office. To this day, the brothers do not speak.

4

The Jame' Asr Hassanil Bolkiah Mosque was stunning: perhaps the most beautiful mosque I'd ever laid my eyes upon. Angela agreed with me. Its massive exterior was finished in pastel blue and white marble, and it was topped with twenty-nine golden domes (because the current Sultan is the 29th). The whole building shimmered in the tropical heat of the morning.

After we'd removed our shoes (and Angela had put on a black body cloak), Jesslyn led us inside. She showed us sparkling fountains and impressive spiralling staircases. Everywhere we looked was white marble. The men's prayer room was particularly magnificent, covered in gold and blue, with a huge chandelier, imported from Austria, dangling in the centre.

Jesslyn told us that she was actually a Buddhist. "But do you want to know something really interesting? My family were once headhunters. Do you know about the headhunters of Borneo?"

Beyond the obvious – that it involved decapitating someone and then keeping the head as some sort of trophy – we told her that we didn't know much about them.

"Many headhunters believed that if they owned another person's head," explained Jesslyn, "then that person would be their slave in the afterlife."

"Whose heads were they?" Angela asked. We were at the exit of the mosque, near where we'd left our shoes.

"Mainly defeated warriors. Heads would be taken by the winning side and brought back to the village to dry."

I looked at Angela. She was grimacing. "So when did headhunting stop?" I asked.

"In the early 19th century. It did not appeal to European values and sensibilities." Jesslyn laughed and looked at me. "Which I am glad for. Headhunting does not appeal to my sensibilities either. But I have pictures of some of my ancestors with heads. I don't know whether to be proud or to be sick."

We put our shoes on and walked to the car. Next stop was the Royal Regalia Building.

5

On the way to the Royal Regalia Building, we passed the grounds of the presidential palace. Jesslyn pointed out the three entrances: one for the sultan, the other for the royal family, and the third for everyone else. We couldn't see much of the palace, unfortunately, because high ground and thick fences had hidden it from view, but we did catch one glimpse of the huge golden dome.

As expected, the Royal Regalia Building was full of royal regalia: royal clothing, royal carriages, royal pictures and royal cushions. Had we been left to our own devices, Angela and I would have covered everything in about ten royal minutes, but with Jesslyn giving us a guided tour it took much longer.

"This museum was established in 1992," explained Jesslyn as we walked towards an admittedly impressive coronation carriage. It was long and black, and embellished with gold. It was definitely fit for a king. "Because 1992 was the year of the sultan's Silver Jubilee."

"And the sultan travelled through the city in this carriage?" Angela asked.

"Yes. He was crowned in 1968 aged 22-years old. Fifty ceremonial soldiers pulled this carriage along the streets of Bandar Seri Begawan. The king was sitting on it the whole time. Look at the throne. It is made from tiger skin."

Upstairs was another large section of the museum. Gifts that the sultan had received from various heads of states, dignitaries and other important people, were displayed in glass cases. Some of the items were impressive, such as a carved wooden lion given by the President of Senegal. The Emir of Qatar had presented a pair of Oryx made from silver and gold, and someone from the United Arab Emirates had offered a diamond-encrusted ceremonial dagger. The Queen of England had presented the sultan with a large crystal glass that must have cost a fortune, and the ruler of Cambodia had handed over an exquisitely-crafted model of Angkor Wat.

The gift from Swaziland was less impressive. It was a few beads tied together to make a necklace. Compared to the other gifts, it looked cheap and nasty. It was obviously much more than that, of course, perhaps an ancient necklace that a tribal chieftain had worn, but to my untrained eye, it looked like a child had made it.

6

"Okay," said Jesslyn. "It is lunchtime, so I will drop you off in the centre of the city. You will easily find a restaurant. And afterwards, you might want to look around some of the shops. I will pick you up in one hour."

Ten minutes later, we were on our own. After changing some Malaysian ringgit into Brunei dollars, we took in our surroundings. Bandar Seri Begawan was not a busy city – that much was clear. Apart from a few cars zipping by, the only people we could see were three Muslim ladies wearing headscarves. We walked along a pristine marble pathway until we arrived at a shopping centre of sorts. In the distance was a massive white and gold mosque.

Though busier than the streets outside, there was still a distinct lack of people inside the shops. We caught an escalator, and after looking around a few shops, found a cafe. We sat and ordered some lunch.

"What do you think of Brunei?" I asked Angela.

"Clean," she answered straightaway, "and orderly."

"Yeah, but where is everyone?"

Inside the cafe with us were a group of veiled teenage girls acting like most teenagers did, laughing as they looked at their iPhones, or posing for photos with mock expressions.

"Maybe everyone is at work. It is Monday," Angela said.

"I tell you one thing I don't like. It's not being able to get a beer." I was referring to the fact that the sale of alcohol was banned in Brunei. "A cold beer on a hot day is one of the great pleasures in life."

7

After lunch, Jesslyn met us again and we walked the short distance to the river. It was busy with small boats crisscrossing each other in what looked like a random manner.

On the other side was Kampong Ayer, a collection of water villages with a population of 30,000. Hundreds of homes were perched on wooden stilts, all serviced by a flotilla of taxi speedboats. As well as residential houses, the water village – which was actually more like a town – had its own schools, mosques, police stations and fuel stations. Extensive plankways and small wooden bridges connected the buildings, all paid for by the sultan.

"He is a very generous man," she told us. "Every year, after Ramadan, everyone can go to his palace and eat there for free – even if they are not Muslim. Afterwards, they can shake hands with him: that is, if they are a man. Women can meet one of his two wives. And every child receives a gift from the king as they leave. Each gets five Brunei dollars."

Unlike the floating village we'd visited in Siem Reap, the buildings of Kampong Ayer were equipped with all the modern amenities needed for life. They had electricity, for a start, and many had modern plumbing and TVs. Internet access was available too. A boat pulled up at a wide wooden jetty, and Jesslyn told us to climb aboard.

"We will travel around the floating village for a while, and then we will visit an actual home. But don't worry; the family is expecting us."

8

The room was spacious, filled with chairs and tables, clearly a place to welcome visitors. On every wall were pictures and photographs of the smiling sultan.

"Please try these offerings," suggested Jesslyn, pointing at the food on the table and gesturing that we should sit down. "This one is roasted banana, and this here is fried wheat." The table had been laid out with various traditional sweet foods for us to try. The middle-aged woman who had prepared them was hovering nearby. Her husband entered the room and poured us some tea.

While Angela watched, I selected an object wrapped in dried mangrove leaves. It was about the length of a pencil, and looked like a green cigar. Jesslyn told me to unwrap the leaves so I could taste the sweet coconut inside. I removed the leaf and found some sort of green jellified paste inside. It wobbled when I shook it, which made me want to gag. With Jesslyn, Angela, and the woman who had made the substance all watching (the husband had disappeared somewhere), I pulled a piece of the green gel off and popped it into my mouth. It was as bad as it looked, like eating a piece of inner tube.

"Mmm," I said, nodding my head, but at the same time placing the remainder on the tray. "Your turn," I said to Angela.

"No thanks," she said, embarrassedly. She looked up at Jesslyn, who was still hovering over us. "I had a big lunch."

"But this lady has produced all this food for you to sample. Please try some."

Angela shook her head. "I'd love to. But I'm just too full. But my husband will try some more, won't you?"

Feeling obliged, I sampled the fried wheat. It was exactly how I imagined shredded wheat cereal must taste after being deep-fried in chip pan oil. Next on the list of delicacies to try was a cube of yellow stuff, which tasted like a cross between a Victoria sponge cake and a piece of old, dog-eared carpet.

"I will show you the kitchen," said Jesslyn. "Come."

It seemed a bit odd wandering through someone's home, especially when we passed a young man and a teenage boy slouched down watching TV. They didn't bat an eyelid as we traipsed past, clearly used to visitors invading their home.

The kitchen was huge. There were five microwaves, a huge food mixer, a dazzling array of pans, endless vats of cooking oil and a large table set out with six chairs. This was where the woman concocted her strange cakes. But why we were being shown the kitchen was anyone's guess. Sometimes it was better not to see where food has been prepared. This was one of those occasions.

"Tomorrow," said Jesslyn, "the woman will be preparing food for one hundred schoolchildren. So today is a quiet day for her. Come, let's go back and finish the food she made for you."

Back in the main greeting room, Angela and I sat down again. I rubbed my stomach in a manner that hopefully suggested I couldn't possibly fit anything else in. Angela glared at me, smiling at the same time. Her look said, *Eat something. Please eat something.*

I picked up the green wobbly thing again and took another bite. As it rolled around on my tongue, I nodded my head in mock appreciation. Then I stuffed another deep-fried shredded wheat down. Just then, we were saved by the arrival of another family of Westerners. Jesslyn said it was time to leave, and so we bowed and thanked the woman.

9

To finish off our whistle-stop tour of Bandar Seri Begawan, Jesslyn drove us to the majestic Omar Ali Saifuddin Mosque, commissioned by the sultan's father. It was a golden-domed building of sheer white-marbled magnificence, easily the most impressive building in the centre of town. Built in 1955, it even had its own lake, complete with a replica of a 16th century royal barge.

We all climbed out of the car and walked to the railings. The barge looked great, but the mosque looked better. According to Jesslyn, the dome was actually covered in pure gold. It must have cost a fortune. After snapping off a few photos, we headed back to the airport to catch our flight back to Kota Kinabalu. One night back at the Rasa Ria, and then it would be time for Bali.

Chapter 15. Last days in Bali

"So, the final stop," I said, as we took our seats on the Air Asia direct flight to Bali. "After nearly seven weeks, we've finally reached the end."

Angela was fastening her seatbelt in preparation for the two-and-a-half hour journey. After adjusting it, she nodded and smiled. "It's been amazing, though, hasn't it? I mean, we've been to places I've only dreamed about before. I never thought I'd ever get to see an orang-utan in the wild, or eat with chopsticks in Japan."

"Or see Angkor Wat in Cambodia and have our feet nibbled by fish in Kuala Lumpur."

Twenty minutes later, we climbed away from the runway, and turned south towards another tropical island.

2

Bali, of course, is the biggest tourist destination in Indonesia. It is a tourist mecca, especially with Australians, but also with Europeans wanting somewhere a bit more exotic than Europe. Our hotel, the Sanur Paradise Plaza, was deliciously touristy, catering for mainly Dutch holidaymakers, but it had a lovely pool, which we intended to lounge next to the following day.

That evening, we wandered the short distance from the hotel to the beach, finding it packed full of locals. In the glorious sun, they were either enjoying the ocean or eating corn-on-the-cob from the food vendors lining the sand. Out in the surf stood three or four fishermen, their conical hats catching the sun as they cast their lines. We also passed a few small Hindu shrines, reminding us that, although Indonesia as a whole was predominantly Muslim, the island of Bali was mainly Hindu. This explained the kites. They were everywhere, both colourful and large, the remnants of the annual kite festival. Bird-like, some hung in the air riding the breeze; others were being carried by eager children.

"This is so nice," said Angela as we watched the sun going down over Sanur Beach. "A great place to end our trip." We headed back to the hotel, content and happy.

3

In 2002, Bali hadn't been so pleasant. On 12th October that year, partygoers had been enjoying a night out in one of the local hot spots when a suicide bomber detonated a device in his backpack. Though this resulted in some structural damage, it was what happened next that caused most of the carnage. As people rushed outside in panic, they began congregating on the street, and it was there that a much more powerful bomb was detonated from a parked car. Most of the 202 fatalities were Western tourists, mainly Australians. In 2008, the Islamic ringleaders of the massacre were executed.

4

Two days later (we had literally done nothing for a whole day, apart from sunbathing and occasionally dipping ourselves in the pool), Angela and I climbed aboard a small but powerful boat for a thirty-minute journey to Lembongan Island, possibly Bali's most appealing retreat. The boat's name was the Barracuda, and as well as us, there were six young Japanese tourists. All of them bowed their heads as we climbed aboard, and when we set off, all sat with impeccable behaviour.

As we approached the island, it wasn't difficult to work out why it was so popular. Clear blue water, exotic palm trees and an unspoilt beach made it an almost perfect tropical island paradise. And the absence of hawkers made it even better.

"There are no roads here," I said to Angela as we waded onto the beach. The Japanese tourists headed away from us, meeting up with a guide who was going to show them around the island. We headed in another direction, towards a bar located on a slight hill.

It afforded us a magnificent view of the Java Sea and coastline – a mesmerising collection of different blues and greens.

While Angela looked in the guidebook for things to do, I took a slurp of my Bintang lager; it hit the spot straight away. I watched as a boat came into shore, not filled with tourists this time, but provisions for the island. A team of locals started unloading boxes and large tins, carrying them up the beach on their heads.

After finishing our drinks, we decided that instead of searching out specific things to see, we would simply walk around, stumbling upon sights as we did so. One thing we couldn't miss were the rows of colourful seaweed laid out on plastic sheets along the shoreline path. Lembongan was famous for its seaweed farms, with rectangular plots clearly visible in the sea. They resembled patchworks of farmers' fields, except in shades of blue and aquamarine instead of green and brown. After being harvested, the seaweed was dried on the plastic sheeting all over the island. Apart from tourism, seaweed farming seemed to be the major contributor to the island's economy.

"They use it in cosmetics," Angela told me. "Bottles of shampoo always say things like: contains seaweed extract."

We walked on, passing a temple, a few stalls, and more drying seaweed, until we arrived at a bar with hammocks instead of chairs. We decided we liked the look of that, and so, for the next hour or so, we read our books, sipped our drinks, and gently swayed to the sounds of water lapping up against a tropical shore.

5

Back aboard the Barracuda, we found out we were the only passengers for the snorkelling trip. The Japanese contingent was still on a tour of the island. They would be getting another boat back to the mainland later on.

As we began motoring out to sea, passing the seaweed farms again, I began to feel apprehensive. I wasn't the strongest of swimmers, especially when my feet couldn't touch the bottom, and I was hardly what you would call a master of the snorkel. In fact, the only other time I'd done it was in the Seychelles. But there, the water had been shallow enough for me to stand up in.

"You'll be fine," Angela said, leaning back in her seat to catch the sun.

"I hope so. It'll be embarrassing if I have to be rescued by the driver."

Ten minutes later, the boat stopped and dropped its anchor. I looked over the side and thought it looked deep. It was as clear as glass, though, and I could see right to the bottom. I wondered if there were any sharks about.

"How deep is it?" I asked the driver, who had just passed me some blue flippers.

"About four metres."

"Any sharks?"

"Maybe."

My heart lurched. "What? Really?"

The driver laughed. "Only joking. No sharks."

Twelve feet still sounded scary, though. There was no way I'd be touching the bottom unless I sank, or a shark dragged me down. I turned to Angela and frowned. She smiled and told me to jump in, and that's exactly what I did.

6

The initial shock of entering the water was the first thing I experienced, closely followed by the mild, but not unexpected, panic at not being able to touch the bottom.

I looked for Angela, who had also jumped in, but she was some way off, splashing away to lure the sharks. Pleased to discover I had some sort of natural buoyancy, I pulled down my mask and plunged my head into the deep. The rush of water up my gullet left me floundering with my flippers kicking and my arms attacking the water. Feeling my heart pounding, I somehow managed to right myself and got my mask and snorkel back into position for a second go. This time, I got it right and what I could see was amazing.

Like most people, I'd seen nature programs on TV showing underwater scenes. I always thought they looked pretty good, but here I was, actually in the water myself. The view was startling. Angela and I were more or less over a coral reef. It was covered with purple and orange organisms, all teeming with tropical fish. Up ahead, I could see Angela's legs kicking, but I couldn't stop staring at the beautiful striped fish beneath me. They were everywhere.

For the next few minutes, I floated about on the surface, occasionally propelling myself with my fins, listening to my own heavy breathing amplified through my mask and snorkel. I could now understand the attraction of scuba diving, and soon forgot that my feet could not touch the bottom. I streamlined my arms next to my body and swam in a way that I thought resembled the Man from Atlantis. I was an expert, the master of the sea. Then I almost choked on another mouthful of seawater.

"Well, I really enjoyed that," I said twenty minutes later. Both of us were lounging about on the top deck of the boat. Other tourist boats were in the general area, and one passed us. It was full to the brim with life-jacketed Westerners. I saw one man staring at us with envy. To him we probably looked like a couple of millionaires on our own private speedboat. And in one way, we were. The trip to the island had cost over a million for the pair of us: 1.3 million Indonesian Rupiah, to be exact (about £90).

7

Sitting in the departure lounge of Denpasar International Airport, waiting for our flight to Amsterdam, and then onto Manchester, Angela and I looked back at some of the photos we'd taken on our trip. Our laptop was full of them. They retraced our steps all the way from Bangkok to Bali.

Angela enlarged a photo of me standing outside a golden stupa in Vientiane. "That seems so long ago," she said, flicking to the next photo of her about to release some birds from a wooden cage.

"So," I said, "what are your top three places?"

Angela flicked through a few more photos – an early morning shot of Da Nang, a photo of us in the Killing Fields, me next to a superhero in Tokyo and Angela lounging in Manila. "I'd still have to say Hong Kong. It just had everything for me – shops, parks, friendly people, tropical trees, and sunny weather. Number two would be maybe...Bangkok. And then probably Phuket. But that might be because of those fish we fed that day. But Kota Kinabalu might be in the top three because of the orang-utans. I don't know. It's so hard to choose. What about you?"

To me, Tokyo was still number one. Just being in the Japanese capital had been exciting. It was as if we'd been in a movie or something – a movie set in the future. But numbers two and three were harder to choose. Phnom Penh had been a worthy stop, because of the Killing Fields and our memorable boat trip. Manila too, though grimy around the edges, had been an interesting stopover. And then there was Halong Bay and Taipei. Each place had offered something new and exciting. My only regret was not being able to see them for longer. Two days here, three days there – our trip around the Far East had been a manic affair. And though we'd traversed vast areas, we'd still missed out huge chunks: China for instance. Not counting Hong Kong and Macau, we hadn't touched the People's Republic of China once. And neither had we visited Korea, either of them. Burma and Singapore were also conspicuous in their absence from our itinerary. All of these would have been great to visit, I felt.

"Okay, I said. Number one is Tokyo. Number two is Bangkok, and number three is Vientiane."

"Vientiane?"

"Yeah. I liked it there. It was quiet and laid-back. And no one ever goes there. That's always a plus in my eyes."

Angela nodded.

Less than one hour later, we were in the sky, heading for Europe.

Macau

Clockwise from top left: Grand Lisboa Hotel and Casino: Senado Square; Busy streets of Macau; Guia Lighthouse; Panorama of downtown Macau; Angela in front of the Ruins of Saint Paul's Cathedral

Tokyo

Clockwise from top left: Senso-ji Buddhist temple and pagoda; Me and Japanese superhero, Ultraman; Tsukiji Fish Market; Wandering around the Imperial Gardens; Shibuya Crossing; Space-age toilet; Mori Tower

Taipei

Clockwise from top left: Confucius Temple; Taipei 101; Downtown Taipei; Martyrs Shrine; Fish Lips in Casserole; Heading to Fisherman's Wharf in Tamsui

Manila

Clockwise from top left: Jeepneys of Manila; Angela with a backdrop of the Pasig River; Andrew, our friend who lives in Manila; Rizal Park; Me in Intramuros

Kuala Lumpur

Clockwise from top left: The Petronas Towers at night; My feet being nibbled by fish; Sultan Abdul Samad Building in Merdeka Square; Batu Caves; Monkey on the Batu Cave Temple steps; One of the Petronas Towers; Inside Bird Park with a lazy stork

Kota Kinabalu

Clockwise from top left: Infant orang-utan; Kota Kinabalu sunset; Atkinson Clock Tower; Me, staring out over the South China Sea; Do you fancy chicken feet and chips, love?; Stilt village near our hotel

Bandar Seri Begawan

Clockwise from top left: Sultan Omar Ali Saifuddin Mosque (note the dome - covered in pure gold); Me in the centre of Bandar Seri Begawan; Jame' Asr Hassanil Bolkiah Mosque; Brunei Dollars; Kampong Ayer

Bali

Clockwise from top left: Sunset falls over Sanur Beach; Hindu Temple in the tropical surrounds of Bali; Angela enjoying the sun aboard the Barracuda; Approaching Lembongan Island (note the seaweed farms in the sea); Boats of Lembongan Island; Seaweed drying in the Southeast Asian sun

If you've enjoyed reading *Temples, Tuk-tuks & Fried Fish Lips*, then perhaps you will want to read other travel books by the same author. All are available on Amazon:

The Red Quest
Flashpacking through Africa
The Balkan Odyssey
Panama City to Rio de Janeiro

Visit **www.theredquest.com** for more details.